SIBLINGS IN DEVELOPMENT

SIBLINGS IN DEVELOPMENT

A PSYCHOANALYTIC VIEW

edited by Vivienne Lewin and Belinda Sharp

Routledge
Taylor & Francis Group
LONDON AND NEW YORK

First published 2009 by Karnac Books Ltd.

2 Park Square, Milton Park, Abingdon, Oxfordshire OX14 4RN
52 Vanderbilt Avenue, New York, NY 10017

Routledge is an imprint of the Taylor & Francis Group, an informa business

First issued in paperback 2019

British Library Cataloguing in Publication Data

A.C.I.P. for this book is available from the British Library

ISBN-13: 978-1-85575-684-7 (pbk)
ISBN-13: 978-0-367-32693-7 (hbk)

Edited, designed, and produced by Sheffield Typesetting
www.sheffieldtypesetting.com
e-mail: admin@sheffieldtypesetting.com

CONTENTS

ACKNOWLEDGEMENTS

We would like to thank Taylor and Francis Ltd, (http://www.informaworld.com) publishers of the *Journal of Child Psychotherapy* for their kind permission to reproduce both Jeanne Magagna's paper "Transformation: from twin to individual", and Margaret Rustin's paper "Taking account of siblings—a view from child psychotherapy". These papers first appeared in Volume 33 no.1 April 2007.

Thanks are also due to Lucy Wilkinson for her transcript of the discussion between Juliet Mitchell and Ronald Britton.

ABOUT THE EDITORS AND CONTRIBUTORS

Ronald Britton was formerly the President of The British Psychoanalytical Society, and the Vice-President of the International Psychoanalytical Association. He is a psychoanalyst in private practice in London and a training and supervising analyst of the BPAS. Publications include Belief and Imagination: Explorations in Psychoanalysis (1998). His latest book is entitled Sex, Death and the Superego (2003).

Prophecy Coles is a Senior Member of the London Centre for Psychotherapy, author of *The Importance of Sibling Relationship in Psychoanalysis* (Karnac, 2003), and editor of *Sibling Relationships* (Karnac, 2006).

Toby Etterley trained at the Anna Freud Centre as a Child and Adolescent Psychotherapist. His professional interests lie particularly with children in the public care and he currently works in a Looked After Children's team in South London and Maudsley NHS Trust; in an independent fostering agency, and in a mainstream infant school.

Before entering into the clinical training Toby worked in a therapeutic community with a group of adolescents and pre-adolescents who had been subjected to sexual abuse.

Vivienne Lewin is a Senior Member of the London Centre for Psychotherapy, Training Therapist, and Supervisor for LCP. She has written several papers on twins in psychoanalytic work, and is the author of a book on the subject, *The Twin in the Transference* (Whurr, 2004—now Wiley).

Jeanne Magagna trained as a Child, Adult and Family Psychotherapist at the Tavistock Clinic in London, and has a doctorate in Child Psychotherapy from University of East London and the Tavistock Clinic. She is Head of Psychotherapy Services and a Consultant Child, Adult and Family Psychotherapist in the Eating Disorders Team at Great Ormond Street Hospital. She is a Consultant Psychotherapist at Ellernmede Centre for Eating Disorders. Jeanne Magagna is the Joint Co-ordinator and Vice-President of the Centro Studi Martha Harris, Tavistock Model Child Psychotherapy Trainings in Florence, Venice, Palermo, Italy. She also teaches infant observation via video link fortnightly with the International Psychoanalytic Institute in Betheseda Maryland. Her work also includes consulting to the organizers and staff group of Family Futures Consortium, an Adoption and Fostering Treatment Centre in London.

Her publications are mainly in the area of eating disorders, psychoses and infant observation. She is the Joint Editor of *Crises in Adolescence* and *Intimate Transformations: Babies with their Families* as well as the Editor of *Universals of Psychoanalysis*. Her publications include *Individual Psychodynamic Therapy in Eating Disorders in Children and Adolescence*, edited by Bryan Lask and Rachel Bryant Waugh (2007).

Juliet Mitchell is Professor of Psychoanalysis and Gender Studies at the University of Cambridge and a full member of the International Society of Psychoanalysis. She has written two books on the subject of Siblings and their place in the inner world: *Mad Men and Medusas: Reclaiming Hysteria and the Effects of Sibling Relationships on the Human Condition* (2000, London, Penguin); and *Siblings* (2003, London, Polity), and she is at work on a third; and several books on feminism and the role of women in psychoanalysis.

Alessandra Piontelli, M.D. is visiting Professor Department of Child Neurology and Psychiatry and Researcher Department of Maternal–Fetal Medicine, University of Milan.

Ellie Roberts is a Child and Adolescent Psychotherapist working for the Oxfordshire and Buckinghamshire Mental Health Trust and in private practice. She teaches on the Tavistock Infant Observation course in Oxford and Bologna.

Margaret Rustin is a Tutor of the Tavistock Child Psychotherapy Training and Head of Child Psychotherapy. She recently gave a series of five lectures, jointly with Michael Rustin, on sibling themes in classic drama. She has co-authored with Michael Rustin *Narratives of Love and Loss* (Verso, 1987), and *Mirror to Nature* (Tavistock/Karnac, 2002), and co-edited *Closely Observed Infants* (Duckworth, 1989), and *Psychotic States in Children* (1997), and *Assessment in Child Psychotherapy* (2000), both published by the Tavistock/Karnac book series.

INTRODUCTION

Vivienne Lewin and Belinda Sharp

This book has emerged from four Conferences held at the London Centre for Psychotherapy in 2007, entitled "Siblings in Development", focussed on the importance of sibling relationships in psychic development. The aim of the conferences was to explore the idea that siblings are not just 2nd editions in relation to the oedipal parents, but have a profound importance in their own right. Relationships with siblings are ineradicably fixed in our psyches. This may become particularly evident at times of stress within the family, when siblings may be especially supportive to each other, or alternately may fall out with intense and lasting bitterness. We may observe this when the parents die and the inheritance of parental valuables creates a powerful dynamic between the siblings. On the one hand, it seems that material inheritance from the parents represents something more than just the goods on offer, as if each child is vying for the favoured place in the parental heart, the most valuable position in relation to the parent. But, in addition, the rivalry between the siblings is about who will inherit the birthright, the mantle of parental power and responsibility.

However, despite our recognition of the psychic importance of siblings, they have been rather neglected in both psychoanalytic theory as regards the metapsychology, and notably in the consulting room, particularly in relation to the transference relationship. Siblings seem to come in and out of focus without ever establishing their structural place in the unconscious dynamic world. As Juliet Mitchell says (Chapter Five), they are everywhere and nowhere, so it seems they cannot really be thought about. Psychoanalytic theory acknowledges the importance of the parental relationship and gives it pride of place in psychoanalytic work, in the many manifestations of the transference. Where, then, do siblings fit it?

We know they play an important part in the development of identity, even for only children. Melanie Klein (1932) wrote of the young child's wish to kill all the babies in mummy's tummy. We know about young children who attempt to smother their baby siblings with love or with hate. Stories about this abound, like a friend whose five-year-old sister set fire to his crib. Fortunately he was rescued in time, unscathed, except by her lifelong hatred of him. In another, a three-year-old boy who, despite not actually having been told that his mother was pregnant, told a visitor that **he** had a baby in his tummy and that because he was a boy, he would push it out through his bottom. He added after a pause, that when he got tired of it, he would push it back into his tummy again.

So, very young children know about what is growing, or potentially growing in mummy's tummy. Only children may long for a sibling, feeling very lonely on their own, or they may relish the superior position they feel themselves to be in, not having to share the parental attention with anyone. Or, as Ron Britton explores in this book (Chapter Five), they may believe they have murdered all the other babies, since there is no other sibling to reassure them that their murderous phantasies have not been enacted. Either way, children are supremely aware of the potential presence of siblings. So we may postulate that just as there is an expectation in the infant that it will have a mother, and a father, there is a parallel expectation that there are/will be siblings. There will be internal representations of siblings in the infant's/child's'/individual's internal world, in the same way as there are internal representations of the parents. Furthermore, these internal siblings would become manifest in the transference relationships that get played out in psychoanalytic work.

The papers in this book are a compilation of the papers presented at the four conferences, and cover a range of approaches and subjects exploring the dynamics between siblings and in the relationships siblings have with others.

The first conference focussed on twins in various settings and circumstances. It began with a report of an observation of twin infants by Toby Etterley, undertaken as part of his clinical training. He observed the "good enough" development of twin girls in their family setting for the first two years of their lives. The twins were dizygotic and, following a difficult labour, were initially separated at birth. The paper illustrates how the parents coped with overwhelming emotions by each "appropriating" a twin for themselves, and cites the projections and over-compensations that they attributed to their infants in the process. He contemplates the idea of symbiotic merger in the relationship between the twins and in fantasy in the parental minds. He highlights the enactment of various twinning scenarios between the parents (and encompassing the observer) and cites the importance of the observation in helping the mother to scaffold the individual developments of her two daughters in her own mind.

Ellie Roberts then presented her work with a twin boy. She described the pre-formed transference and subsequent development of the transference of a five-year-old twin presenting with developmental delay. The work shows how the consulting room was used as an intrauterine place, showing an enmeshment with the twin inside his mother. The child demonstrated his worry of emerging into the world and how he developed an interest in God to help with the loneliness he began to feel. The material touched on Meltzer's concept of the aesthetic conflict.

We had planned that Professor Alessandra Piontelli would present her work on ultra-sound scans of twins in utero, but unfortunately she was unable to attend the conference due to personal circumstances. However, we were more than compensated for this disappointment by a presentation by Jeanne Magagna of an observation of conjoined twins and the emotional consequences of their separation. Conjoined twins are rare, and seldom survive long enough to be separated. So we were privileged to hear a detailed account of an observation of the twins both before and after separation. This proved to be a very emotive paper, in part because the material was sometimes very painful, but also, perhaps, indicating something about our deepest phantasies about personal and individual identity and aloneness.

Vivienne Lewin then followed with a reading of the introductory chapter of her book on twins and the twin relationship, focusing on the importance of the twin in the transference. An expanded version of this chapter is included in the book.

The second conference focused on all siblings, beginning with a discussion between Juliet Mitchell and Ron Britton about the place of siblings in psychoanalytic theory and practice. The discussion encompassed an exploration of the internal framework for individual development and the place for siblings in this, both in our own culture and that in others. They also considered what we might learn about our own psychical structure from the practices in other cultures. A report on this discussion appears in Chapter Five.

Prophecy Coles presented her work on the subject of sibling incest. She addressed the question as to the possible causes for sibling incest. She looked at the emotional consequences on both the perpetrator and the victim, and she finally speculated about the frequency of sibling incest and commented upon the dearth of papers in the psychoanalytic literature.

In Conference 3, two papers were presented: the first was by Jeanne Magagna on her work with an adolescent twin girl. This paper considers aspects of sibling relationships, explored in the course of both individual and family psychotherapy. The case material presented included various aspects of work with a twin emerging from a merged state with her twin sister towards the development of a sense of identity as an individual.

Margaret Rustin presented her paper on siblings from the point of view of child psychotherapy. This paper argues that child psychotherapy has a long tradition of interest in sibling relationships and she described the significant contributions in this tradition. She discussed possible sociological factors in the current psychoanalytic focus on siblings, and went on to review, briefly, psychoanalytic theorizing of siblinghood. The core of the paper uses observational clinical and literary material to describe different forms of sibling relationship, both real and imagined. She also made brief reference to the issue of lost siblings. She argued that siblings are always part of our inner world whether we have actual siblings or not. Margaret also responded to the observational material in Jeanne Magagna's paper, to open up a dialogue. The conclusion of her paper draws attention to the complex mix of sibling ambivalence—siblings are likely to be the prototype of both our best friends and our worst enemies among peers—and raises the question of what to make of the traditional concept of "the brotherhood of man", a subject also discussed by Ron Britton and Juliet Mitchell in Chapter Five.

We were fortunate that Allessandra Piontelli was able to come to present her work at a separate morning conference. Chapter Nine is a report of this conference. Professor Piontelli began by describing the intrauterine behaviour of twin foetuses and dispelling some common myths attached to it. Subsequently birth, prematurity, and favouritism impact on the family, and the nascent link between the twins was described and illustrated by video material. Twins in other cultures were also discussed. Professor Piontelli suggested that twins are extremely taxing and family life is disrupted by their birth to an unusual degree. Mothers generally favour one and, due to ultrasound-graphic images, this choice is often made from before birth. Fathers may be overwhelmed. Siblings can be extremely jealous but a few take pride in the twins and help in their care. Twins seem to be aware of each other from birth and initially compete for their mother's attention. Professor Piontelli added that the first signs of mutual recognition start at around four months. From then on the co-twin becomes an increasingly important presence in each twin's life. Some twins, however, are more compatible than others who continue to manifest irritation, competition and jealousy towards each other. Twins illustrate the importance of siblings' relationships to an unusual degree.

We hope that as a result of both the conferences, and the publication of this book of papers from the conferences, siblings and the metapsychology relating to them will remain more in focus in psychoanalytic work. This will, of course, mean that more attention will be paid to the sibling transference, and we hope therefore that this book will make a significant contribution to understanding the depth and meaning of our relationship with our siblings.

CONFERENCE 1

CHAPTER ONE

When two become four: A two-year observation of dizygotic twin infant girls in their family setting

Toby Etterley

> "All Fords are exactly alike, but no two men are just alike. Every new life is a new thing under the sun; there has never been anything just like it before, never will be again." (Henry Ford)[1]
>
> "There are two things in life for which we are never truly prepared: Twins." (Josh Billings)[2]

Introduction

Liz and David were a very warm, affable married couple living in suburban London. They were both Caucasian in origin, in their early thirties and university educated. Though they worked in quite different spheres, creativity and the arts were highly valued by both of them—personally and professionally. I made contact with them through a mutual acquaintance who informed me that the couple were having twins, that this was their first pregnancy, and that they were keen to participate in a mother–infant(s) observation. Liz was in the 36th week of pregnancy when I first went to meet her and David. They greeted me warmly, and after mutual introductions Liz patted her (very large) bump and said, "And these are the twins."

During this meeting I learned that there was no history of multiple births in either Liz or David's families. Moreover, due to a late first scan, they had only discovered that they were having twins at 20 weeks gestation. Liz's pregnancy had been a good one, though there was a recent (and as it turned out founded) concern that she had pre-eclampsia, a disorder that can be highly dangerous to both mother and infant(s).

Liz was (perhaps unsurprisingly) anxious and overwhelmed in this introductory meeting. She talked of how they were having twins and yet they had no experience as parents. She also revealed her concerns that due to this condition she might now be damaging her unborn babies. She said, "I just want them out now," and added that there was nothing that she could do for them whilst they were "inside". She said that once they were born she and David would know if they were okay and would be able to comfort them if they weren't.

In this first meeting, and even before the twins were born, there was a sense of a couple working together and as a unit. David stayed and acted as a "gatekeeper", as he often did in later observations (as he worked from home). He asked practical questions about the observation—what I was looking for, how it would work, how regularly I would need to come etc? After this he left us (and returned to decorating the nursery). Liz informed me that whilst they had wanted to, they hadn't been able to find out the sex of the babies. She added that she was, however, sure that at least one of them was a boy and would be "very surprised" if they were both girls. Liz's certainty about this was striking and remained unclear. Although inevitably multi-faceted, I came to understand that the issue of difference and differentiation was a central one for Liz and a fundamental factor in the decision to admit an observer to such a special and private period of their lives. Indeed, later on when reflecting back on the observations Liz said,

"It's strange but it gives me a space to think back over the girls' weeks and to think about their development and the differences between them." She also told me of identical twin boys she had known as a child and how they were always dressed alike and treated as if they were two copies of the same person. I had the sense that this story conveyed a fundamental anxiety of Liz's—would she have the space in her mind to meet these two new individuals as such?

"Divide and conquer!" – meeting "the girls"

I first met Katie and Jo when they were 26 days old. On my journey to the house I became increasingly aware of my own doubts and concerns over my ability to observe two infants simultaneously. I was worried about how it would work out practically and excited at the prospect of finally meeting them. My fears seemed to have been realized when I finally arrived at the house. David greeted me telling that Liz was over at the shops but was aware that I was coming. As we stood in the hallway David pointed toward a recliner on the lounge floor and said, "One's in there" and then toward another recliner on his study floor and added, "...and one's in there!" He exclaimed, "It's divide and conquer today!" I realised that each baby was settled next to a speaker and that soft relaxing music was playing in the background. I felt momentarily thrown, feeling that I had to choose one infant over the other and aware that I couldn't really see either from my current position.

David now beckoned me through to the lounge and carefully carried the recliner from the study through saying, "This is Jo." He then motioned toward the other baby adding, "...and this is Katie". He placed the babies side by side in front of the sofa and said, "There, now you can see them both." I smiled and took them in, immediately being drawn to the differences between them.

26 days

> I stood looking at the two infants. Both were still sleeping. Jo seemed to be in a less deep sleep. Her left arm was held straight outward and her right arm was by her side. Her left hand slowly opened and closed, pausing in each position before repeating the movement. She seemed to be experiencing the difference between skin touching

> skin and then not touching anything. Her right hand was cupped, almost into a fist but not as tight. The ends of her fingers were lightly touching the palm of her hand. Her face and mouth were also in constant motion. Her eyes remained shut.
>
> Katie lay with both her elbows bent and her forearms held upward. Her right hand was inside her sleeve and not visible. Her left hand was cupped in a similar way to Jo's right hand. Her eyes seemed shut more tightly than Jo's and her face expressionless and still. Her head was bowed and most of her mouth and chin was hidden beneath the top part of her dungarees. She appeared to have the material of her dungarees between her lips but was not sucking. I noticed that their faces were very different. Jo was also physically bigger. Neither had a lot of hair, though Katie's scalp almost resembled a shaven head and was darker in colouration than the very fair strands of hair on Jo's head.

I was very aware of my anxiety about mixing them up, whether I would be able to tell them apart if they were moved from their positions on the floor and whether I would be able to hold onto the detail that I was observing. Indeed, on leaving the observations I used to urgently speak into a Dictaphone, not trusting my own mind to hold onto the mass of material.

I had been aware that there had been some complications around the births and David informed me that whilst Katie's birth had been very straightforward, Jo's delivery (17 minutes later) was a very different matter. He explained that she had been in a transverse position across the top of the womb and had to be delivered with the aid of forceps. However, she didn't start breathing naturally and had to be resuscitated. Jo subsequently had to be taken to the special care baby unit (SCBU), whilst Katie had remained with Liz in a completely different part of the hospital. David described how torn he had felt and added that Liz had felt very guilty, as she wasn't physically able to get to see Jo initially. Later on the hospital staff had suggested that Liz take Katie home and leave Jo in the SCBU to complete her course of antibiotics. David added with some pride that Liz had refused to come home with only one of the girls.

In contrast with this striving for togetherness I was struck by David's sense that this twin unit had still to be physically divided—wrenched apart and defeated. I wondered about the battle in his "divide and conquer". Was he harbouring a sense of rivalry or envy at their closeness, at the exclusive and hidden experiences that they had shared together in utero? It also occurred to me later that perhaps there was a concern about each twin's individuality and uniqueness—did they need to be kept apart to exist as individuals? Indeed, on her return Liz described her daughters as "the girls" and told me that they were going to avoid calling them "the twins". She added that she understood that this could lead to resentment in later life "due to each child not being seen as an individual". As if responding to the anxiety aroused by this thought, she said that she was beginning to be able to discern one baby's crying from the other and to understand the communication behind at least some of their cries.

Liz wondered about their experience of twinning—were they aware of one another and of the fact that they were sisters? It struck me that she was pondering the symbiotic aspects of twinship (both for them and for her). She went on to talk of them almost as one, wondering whether I had noticed how long their fingers were and adding that David felt that they were going to be pianists when they were older.

What became increasingly apparent, even at this early stage, was how the process of differentiation in the parental minds involved an over-compensation for Jo. For example, Liz said that Jo was much more aware and expressive than Katie. She and David felt that she was the more developmentally advanced twin and believed that she was actually conceived first. Both parents also commented that they felt that Katie had looked more like a baby who should have been in the SCBU as she was somewhat smaller than her sister.

Additionally, and as the following vignette illustrates, Liz seemed to resort to a defensive denial against the pain of this traumatic beginning.

> Jo was still sleeping and began to stir, both arms moving around a little more frantically. She pulled a face resembling a grimace. Liz placed her left hand gently on Jo's tummy saying, "You like that, don't you." Jo's eyes remained shut. Liz said that she wondered what babies dreamt about. She said that dreams, as she understood them, were a way of working things out, but what could a baby possibly have to work out? She said that she knew about the baby's tongue and sucking movements in its sleep and that it was imagining a feed, but she couldn't understand what other experiences they had to draw upon.

There was an unspoken anxiety about Jo's traumatic birth—the experience that she did have to draw upon or might need to work out. Soon after this interaction Liz looked at Jo and said, "You're perfect, aren't you?" and I had the sense that this was both an affirmation and a question. Later in this same observation Jo suddenly froze, her eyes staring blankly up at the ceiling when Liz placed her on the changing table. Liz responded initially by saying, "Look at you!" and then quickly lowered her right ear to Jo's mouth to check that she was still breathing. I was struck by Jo's response; what could it mean? Had the cold changing table been reminiscent of the early, traumatic hospital experience? However, equally striking was Liz's response; the sense of precariousness that surrounded Jo's "going on being" and the unspoken terror associated with this. In my seminar group fears of long-term brain damage were raised (though proved unfounded).

In this early visit I also learned that whilst Liz was breast-feeding Katie, Jo was being bottle-fed. It wasn't clear how supportive the hospital staff had been in helping to try and establish breast-feeding in such difficult circumstances. However, Liz's ambivalence around this development was clear as she said that she wasn't sure how much difference breast-feeding made. She also noted that actually the bottle-fed Jo was a lot bigger than her breast-fed sister and added that the main difference probably wasn't a nutritional one but instead concerned the quality of the feed. She said that anyone could feed Jo whilst only she could feed Katie. However, following this admission she quickly said that, of course, it did make feeding two babies somewhat easier.

Breast-feeding never took place during any of my observations and on my fourth visit I learned that Liz was supplementing Katie's feeds with a bottle, maintaining her breast-feeds only at night. The rationale for this was that Liz had an insufficient milk supply, though I wondered about the impact of having a male observer, in addition to having a twin who was being exclusively bottle-fed. Though there is insufficient space within this paper to fully explore the significance of my gender, I feel that it was a further focus of rivalry, competition and twinning.

Due to the difficulties around the birth and the early separation, Katie's first week post-partum was spent with mother as a singleton, whilst Jo was in an incubator. In my seminar group we wondered about Liz's guilt at "choosing" one baby over the other in addition to the sudden rupture experienced by Katie and Jo and the huge contrast in their early lives. Liz commented on how David was "more natural" with the girls than she was and said that she didn't know how anyone coped with twins on their own.

Jo seemed to be endowed as a "daddy's girl" and as rejecting of the symbiotic closeness with her mother ("she refused the breast"). Liz talked about how it had been Jo who had kicked her inside the womb as it was she who was lying across the top and there was a sense in which she felt that Jo was still kicking her on the outside ("She doesn't want me, she wants food"). I also wondered if something competitive between the parents was being played out with the girls (another kind of twinning relationship).

As an extension of this, the parental attributions ascribed to Jo centred upon her size, strength, activity, and outgoing nature, all very masculine characteristics. It struck me that the diminutive of her name by which she was known was a rather boyish one, in contrast to her sister's very feminine name. Katie meanwhile was smaller and seen as more fragile and generally more passive. Similarly, Liz's twinning with this infant seemed apparent as she described an interaction where Katie had turned away from her sister when they were lying on the play-mat together. Liz added that maybe Katie had been angry that Jo had taken up all of the room in the womb. It struck me that the parental projection toward Katie seemed to be that she too, like her mum, had had to suffer Jo's kicks.

The first 6 months

As the early weeks went by I was struck that Katie would have more physical holding from her mother, and also that their contact seemed more sensual. For the first eight weeks Jo was generally with her father and often in his study when I arrived and was quickly brought into the lounge with Liz's insistence that, "Toby comes to observe both of the girls, not just one of them." During this time I noticed that Katie seemed to sleep much more heavily than her sister and I wondered whether this was a developed response to being with a more active twin in utero. However, whilst Jo seemed an innately more physical baby, I wondered to what extent this might have been a reflection of (and in response to) the different quality of mothering that she was experiencing. Indeed, in this early period it seemed as if David undertook the "environment mothering" for Jo and he would feed, carry, and soothe her whilst Liz dealt with Katie. However, the first feed that I observed David giving Jo felt quite distressing and very different from her twin's experience.

5 weeks

> Jo's tongue began to protrude from her mouth and it looked like it was making circling motions inside. David carefully put the teat to her lips and she hungrily took it and began sucking vigorously. She looked up at David's face and he awkwardly picked up a newspaper and opened it out on the coffee table in front of him. He didn't return Jo's gaze but instead began to read, occasionally commenting on a story and reading it aloud. Some of Jo's milk began to spill out of her mouth and down her cheeks and he did not notice and did not wipe it away. I felt very moved as Jo continued to gaze up at his preoccupied face.
>
> ...Liz was far more attentive to Katie. She gazed at Katie as she sucked and gently stroked her head. Katie gazed up at Liz and her body stilled. She moved her cupped hands in toward her body and placed them together under her chin... Jo continued sucking vigorously and looking upward. At one point she held her right hand up, as if seeking attention. David took hold of her hand between his thumb and forefinger but did not make eye contact with her.

I was struck by how Katie seemed so much more possessive with her eyes, as if she really grabbed her mother and drew her in with them. In contrast, the active Jo seemed to become much more passive during her feeds and needed to work much harder physically to grab her object. Indeed, later in this same observation as David stood over a crying Jo, he commented: "Its amazing how quickly you get immune to a baby's cry, particularly when you know that they just want physical proximity." Although very competent and clearly aware of her communications, David was preoccupied with other things. It seemed that Jo, more than her sister, had to compete with a twin for her object's attention. Her "environment mothering" in these early weeks, whilst good enough, lacked the emotional intensity of her sister's and had a much more practical or rudimentary feel to it.

A number of weeks later I observed a particularly intense feeding interaction between Katie and her mother, in addition to a simultaneous feed between Jo and her father.

9 weeks

> Katie showed some delight, moving her arms and legs as Liz put the teat of the bottle to her mouth. She hungrily took it and sucked frantically a few times. She stilled and her sucking slowed to a more rhythmic pace, her heavy breathing interrupting the pattern periodically. Katie gazed up at Liz, who smiled back at her. Liz maintained her eye contact with Katie and they gazed at each other for some time before Liz said,: "Why don't you look at Toby. You see my face all the time." I looked closely at this pair, who seemed completely lost in one another. Liz had a smile on her face and was clearly enjoying being the centre of Katie's world.
>
> Jo lay across David's knees, her bottom and lower back poking through the gap in his legs so that his thighs supported her head and knees. She looked less securely held than her sister but was sucking steadily and rhythmically from her bottle. Her arms were by her sides and both of her hands were closed, forming loose fists. She and David were similarly gazing at one another, though David periodically broke away to look over at the television.

On the completion of Katie's feed Liz looked up and apologised to me, as if suddenly roused from the mutual state of reverie, and perhaps relating to me as the excluded twin. Liz said that Katie "did this" when someone else was present or when the TV was on. She added that when they were alone together Katie would often look around the room and not at her. It was unclear to what extent this report was based upon a parental projection of competition or exclusion—a getting rid of the other and the associated guilt. Certainly at times it seemed almost as if Liz and David were transformed into a pair of twins as issues of rivalry and competition in particular were played out between them.

However, I also wondered how each of the twins experienced the contrast between the presence and the absence of the other, a primitive sense of absence or incompleteness. Knight (cited in Orr, 1941) states that a twin alone feels "half an individual", whilst Steinfeld (cited in Orr, 1941) refers to two twins together experiencing themselves as forming "only one organism". During these early weeks and months it seemed as if Jo reached out to her sister more. She also seemed far more reactive to Katie's affective states and the parents reported that Katie would sleep through Jo's crying at night, whilst Katie's crying would wake her sister. David, in particular, attributed something malicious to Jo, citing her pleasure at her sister's distress. It seemed as if David's ambivalence and even hostility about having twins were projected into Jo, and I wondered whether at such times he became twinned with her against this rival other. He would make the occasional cutting joke and comment saying, for example, that they should, "Put Katie back up the chimney" or telling me, "We got rid of the other one" when I arrived to find only Jo in the lounge.

In contrast I actually had the sense that Jo was very much attuned to her sister's distress in a way that Katie didn't appear to be. I felt that perhaps Jo experienced her sister's cries on a very symbiotic level as an extension of her own. Indeed, Liz often reported how Jo would stop crying when Katie started. At such times, and especially at night, I had the sense that the girls became one enormous crying baby in Liz's mind in the manner that Davison (1992) reports.

A significant change took place at 14 weeks as I arrived to discover Jo occupying her mother's lap, a place that she increasingly shared with Katie hereafter. Perhaps in response to this change Katie became particularly unsettled at night. This solution seemed to have a particularly beneficial outcome for her as she was subsequently removed from her shared cot and taken to the spare room with Liz so that the others could sleep.

At 20 weeks Liz returned to her job on a part-time basis (working four mornings per week) to work out her two-month notice period. David looked after the girls during this time and the impact of the loss of mother seemed to be felt much more profoundly by Katie. The following vignette took place in an observation shortly after Liz's return to work.

20 weeks

> Jo and Katie were under the baby gym on the floor mat side-by-side. Jo bent her legs and lifted them right up toward the hanging objects. She made contact with one of the rings and stopped as it rattled. She lowered her legs and then repeated the action, though didn't catch anything this time. Katie seemed to have been watching this and

> lifted her head and legs up toward the hanging objects at the same time. She then looked at me, lowered her head and began to cry in quite a distressed way. Katie turned away from Jo and began to cry with even more distress. Jo raised her right arm again and reached by her side, lowering it so that her arm rested on Katie's head. Jo turned her head and looked at Katie who continued to look away.

Jo certainly seemed less unsettled by Liz's return to work, perhaps because of David's continued presence. In contrast, Katie seemed to regress somewhat and to become much more clingy. I also had the sense that my presence was felt as much more threatening to her in some way, perhaps relating to me as a rival twin with whom she had to compete for her object's attention. Liz felt very guilty about her return to work and strongly conveyed her sense that she was really missing out on important developments in the girls' lives. Her struggle with her own sense of loss seemed to make it harder for her to deal with Katie's regression. She appeared to be somewhat agitated by it and seemed keen to push Katie to be more active (and presumably robust) as her sister was felt to be.

For a short while during my visits Katie, Jo and Liz seemed to have negotiated a solution whereby one baby slept whilst the other had exclusive access to mother. At other points when both twins were awake and unsettled I was sometimes pulled from my neutral observer's stance by Liz asking if I minded giving one of the girls a cuddle or even just rocking a chair with my foot. This felt like a testing of both me and my boundaries, in addition to a coupling with me. At other times it seemed to be simply an expression of the impossibility of meeting the needs of two infants simultaneously. A new theme of fairness now entered the observations, Liz being keen to ensure that neither baby was left behind or left out. New accomplishments by one twin were, however, always greeted by a comparison with the other. As if they had read the script, Jo's first tooth appeared just before she was six months old and Katie developed the very same tooth the very next day.

The emergence of Tigger and Pooh (6 to 12 months)

David gradually, and almost imperceptibly at first, began to withdraw from the observations. This seemed to coincide with, or was perhaps the springboard for, Liz's growing competence in managing both of the girls. At six months old the twins faced two major separations as they were moved out of the parental bedroom and into the nursery and, shortly afterwards, out of their shared cot and each into their own. These moves seemed to coincide with a further separation between them in Liz's mind as she said, "I think they're starting to look quite different to one another again." She added that they had looked quite different initially and then had started to look more alike. Liz looked at Katie and said, "I think you take after my family" and then said to Jo, "You definitely take after daddy's family."

At about this time bouncers that could be hung in the doorway were introduced. The active Jo particularly took to these with great aplomb, leading the parents to identify her with the bouncy Tigger from Winnie-the-Pooh. Liz and David seemed to relish their own rediscovered space, taking their first weekend away whilst the twins stayed with their maternal grandparents. Liz seemed to be quite active in propelling Katie and Jo toward a realisation of their separateness from one another in addition to their separateness from her. However, perhaps in response to her own guilt about this she was quick to say that the girls hadn't even noticed that they had gone and drew back on their tie to one another by telling me that their travel cots had been in a room together as their own cots were at home.

As if trying on different aspects of self and other, the girls would often seem to swap roles and attributes. For example, Jo now grizzled and Katie reached out and took her hand, babbling away to her as if comforting her unsettled sister. Katie now seemed to become more active, perhaps propelled by the anxiety surrounding the recent separations. She had mastered sitting up before her sister and seemed more ready to crawl. As if still over-compensating for Jo, Liz commented that previously it had seemed as if "Jo was better at everything", but now Jo was better at some things and Katie was better at others. Concern lingered around Jo as she was referred to a paediatrician due to having an oddly shaped head and particularly high forehead. Though Liz attended the appointments, she remained adamant that nothing was wrong with Jo and was disdainful when she was proved right.

The issue of fairness remained a central one, particularly around mealtimes when Liz would count the number of spoonfuls each twin had had. As Davison (1992) highlights, the presence of another hungry mouth meant that there was less time to mess around with food. It also seemed that having to witness her sister being fed did produce a certain amount of impatience in each twin that was not motivated by hunger alone, as evidenced in the following vignette.

30 weeks

> Liz sat down on a chair between the two girls. Jo began to grizzle and waved her right arm in the air. Liz offered a spoonful of food to Jo, who greedily took it, closing her mouth and spilling some of its contents down her chin. She then began making a chewing motion followed by a sucking action. She opened her mouth again and looked up at Liz, who offered her another spoonful. Liz repeated this three more times, counting how many spoonfuls Jo had had before turning to Katie. Katie took the first spoonful a little more hesitantly and then screwed her face up as she tentatively chewed and then sucked its contents. Katie took the next few spoonfuls that were offered to her in a similar way, her face screwing up after each mouthful, and much of its contents dribbling down her chin and having to be rescued by Liz.
>
> As Liz offered the fourth spoonful, Katie turned her mouth away. Liz offered it again and Katie kept her head turned away and her mouth closed. Jo was being very vocal and reaching out in Liz's direction and Liz now turned to her. Liz fed her another few spoonfuls and Katie began to hit the tray area of her highchair with her spoon, grasping it firmly in the clenched fist of her right hand. Liz returned to Katie and fed her another few mouthfuls. Katie reacted in the same manner as before, eating the food and then screwing her face up. Katie again protested as Liz gave the remaining contents to Jo and then got up to fetch dessert.

I had the sense in this observation that Katie didn't really want the food, yet more than this she didn't want her sister to have it or mother. Her impatience and her complaint, therefore, seemed more about the attention that she wasn't getting rather than the food that Jo was.

As the first summer break approached Liz's attachment to me was evident as she joked that I would "miss the girls walking and talking and everything". Sure enough Katie began to crawl during the second of my four-week break. On my return I was struck by Liz's frustration at Jo's lack of mobility. Both she and David seemed keen to push the girls on toward independence and had enrolled them in a nursery for one day per week. Liz talked about her need for own time and became involved in some private consultancy work on this day. The role fluidity between the girls continued, as Katie now became the more active and outgoing twin, taking on the Tigger mantle. Competition and rivalry between them seemed increasingly apparent as both twins now clearly showed a preference for Liz.

51 weeks

> The twins were downstairs with David in the living room. Liz now came down the stairs and Katie walked over to meet her with the baby walker. Liz had to squeeze through the gate, as Katie was standing right in front of it. Liz looked at her and said, "Hello Pickle, are you going to let me through?" Jo looked up and now began shuffling toward the hall on her bottom. She sat in the lounge doorway and held her arms up. Liz smiled and picked Jo up. Katie looked up at Jo and began to grizzle. Liz said, "Come this way then Katie" as she came into the lounge. Liz sat on the floor and sat Jo on her knee. Katie approached Liz and was picked up and cuddled on the other knee, Jo looking to her sister and Katie burying her face in Liz's chest as if to block out the other.

Though Liz had by now found the space in her lap for two girls Katie seemed to continue to block out her sister at such moments, as if to maintain the illusion of her exclusive intimacy with her mother. At other times the girls would actively shove each other in an attempt to free mother's lap of the impostor.

The second year

As we moved into the second year of the observation I reduced my visits to fortnightly. This seemed to be a particular issue for Liz who began to comment "Two weeks is such a long time that I can't remember" as she sought to update me on the twins' individual developments. Katie too seemed somewhat slower in her response to me whilst Jo continued to relate to me quite actively. David was now often out when I visited as he became preoccupied in building up his business. I felt that my observations had helped Liz to become more competent and solid in her role as the mother of twins. However, perhaps seeking to fill the gap left by my reduction Liz found and joined a twins club. This seemed to provide her with a narcissistic gain, reinforcing her pride in her different social status and allowing her to identify with a group of peers in a relationship that approximated another sibship or even twinship (Leonard, 1961).

Walking became the new source of rivalry and competition, not least in the parental minds. Katie launched herself into it wholeheartedly at a little over a year old and Liz congratulated her, "You're the best walker in the house, aren't you Pickle?" I began to notice that Liz did not now add a parallel complement to Jo as she had done constantly before. Katie was certainly the dominant and more articulate twin and Jo often followed her, both literally and developmentally. It seemed as if Jo often backed out of the competition with her sister, and as Katie grew more cheeky and defiant with Liz, Jo resorted instead to a more regressed relating to her mother. As the twins continued the task of separation and individuation, the issue of loss obviously become a particularly poignant one for them, as the following vignette reveals.

20 months

> Jo and Katie were each sitting on a cushion on the lounge floor watching Telly Tubbies. They were both very engaged with the TV and each made noises, "Uh oh" and pointed at the screen. In the story there was a strong wind that came and blew away all the Telly Tubbies' possessions. They were hanging in the air but could not be reached. Jo particularly pointed at the lost objects, her mouth open. She said something that I couldn't understand and was clearly upset. Liz came in and Jo turned around and looked at Liz before pointing back at the TV. Katie said, "All gone" and Jo replied, "Uh oh!" Liz said that it was sad but that she was sure they would get them back. Jo continued to point at the TV and Liz said, "I know Pickle" and then said again that they would come back. Gradually the wind died down and the possessions returned one by one. Katie clapped and Jo joined in with this.

Jo seemed to have a far greater preoccupation with loss than her sister and seemed to be trying to work something through. She had a good capacity for imaginary play and later in this observation she sat under her highchair and held onto the strap. Gazing upwards and swaying from side to side she said, "Jo fly kite." Liz smiled and acknowledged that she was flying her kite like the Telly Tubbies and Jo nodded and continued. I had the sense that loss for her represented something that she wanted from her mother and felt that that she hadn't got, perhaps the early intimacy that she had missed out on and was trying to recapture now.

21 months

> Jo reached out and touched Liz's breast, her forefinger pointing directly at it. Liz asked what she wanted and Jo continued to point and said, "juice". Liz said that she had her beaker. Jo continued to point at Liz's breast and Liz offered her a sip of her own water. Jo sipped from the glass and the water trickled down her chin.

Jo now seemed to be making more demands of the breast/mother that had perhaps been felt to be lacking in her earlier development. Liz seemed to pick up on this intuitively and responded by giving Jo additional support and making adaptations to meet her regressive needs in the moment.

As the final few months wore on there were some ongoing signs of confusion between "me" and "not me" in the manner that Burlingham (1952) reports. This seemed particularly so for Jo who, for example, reacted as if she had been hurt when Katie fell and hurt herself. Yet as Katie increasingly identified with Tigger and jumped around saying, "I can bounce!" Jo turned to a soft cuddly Eeyore toy. His increasing appearance and importance indicated that separation and individuation were well under way and he seemed to serve as a transitional object, accompanying Jo wherever she went. Her good enough maternal care was evident as she fed him, changed his nappy and tenderly put him to bed with a kiss and a cuddle. However, I was struck by her identification with this rather sad, hapless soul.

Though Jo became somewhat more defiant I did wonder to what extent Katie communicated the more sadistic and challenging qualities for her sister as well as herself. Indeed, whilst Katie continued jumping on the sofa and saying, "Yes" in response to Liz's "No", Jo stood shaking her head at the tenacity of her "naughty" sister. I was struck that Katie seemed to be more securely in the omnipotent narcissistic phase of development and much more separate from both her sister and her mother. Though the girls played together with delight, often chasing one another with the confirmatory "Jo chase Katie" or "Katie chase Jo", it was often (though not always) Katie who led the way in such activity and Jo who followed.

As our final meeting arrived I approached the house with a very different sense of trepidation from my first visit. Liz had been talking about the ending of the observations for some time and this separation was clearly a significant one for her. She acknowledged how much the observations had helped her and even sought to bypass an ending by suggesting that I could continue to see the family socially. The working through of a clear and planned ending seemed to help Liz in her grieving process around the loss of her "fantasy son" and she announced that she and David had decided that they weren't going to have any more children and that their family was full enough.

The ending was an incredibly sad one but I watched with real joy and pleasure as the girls lay on the lounge floor together peering through the curtains of the puppet theatre with David. The puppet theatre had been my parting gift for the twins' second birthday and they giggled conspiratorially as they each chose their puppets. Katie then held her bird puppet aloft saying, "Birdie flying" and Jo took to the stage with her giraffe saying, "Giraffe walking". They laughed with glee as Liz, David and I applauded this little production.

Discussion

The term "symbiosis" was utilised by Mahler (1952) to describe the very primitive stage in the development of a child during which his identity is fused with that of his mother. Up to the age of six to eight months Mahler stated that infants could not readily distinguish between that which belonged to his mother and that which was a part of him. Many authors have since applied the concept of symbiosis to twins. As Freud and Dann (1951) originally pointed out, followed by Leonard (1961) and Dibble & Cohen (1981), the first object for a twin—the object whose immediate and constant presence is most total—is, in fact, not the mother but the other twin. They argue that due to this fundamental fact twin–twin symbiosis at least competes with, if not supplants, each infant's symbiotic union with the mother. In addition, mother is seen as a figure that disturbs twinly symbiosis and presents herself as an object that excites rivalry between the twins for her favours. In this model the symbiotic relationship between the twins appears to be equivalent to the symbiotic relationship between infant(s) and mother. It strikes me that David seemed to have a similar, though somewhat harsher, version of this story in his mind when he said, "It's divide and conquer today"; the competition for a share of the twinly symbiotic union instead being turned into a conquering and defeating of it.

Other authors such as Stern (1985) have proffered that in normal development infants do not experience a period of self-other undifferentiation. By extension there would be no place for twin–twin symbiosis within this model. In a midway point between these perspectives, Piontelli (1989) draws upon observations of dizygotic twins in utero and states that certain temperamental characteristics are continuous through the pre- and post-natal periods. She perceives the "psychological birth" of an infant to be a highly individual matter. She states that some children seem to show evidence of psychological awareness long before birth, whilst others seem to refuse to be psychologically born long after the caesura of birth.

I had the sense that for the twins described here, just as for singletons, the most avidly searched for and depended upon object was ultimately the mother. However, it struck me that the twinly symbiotic pull would emerge particularly in the absence of this object. Moreover, it seemed to be far stronger for Jo than for her sister, undoubtedly due in no small measure to the different environmental conditions and care she experienced post-partum and in her early weeks. Athanassiou (1986) states that the symbiotic aspect of the twin relationship may be greater in monozygotic twins, but is encouraged or otherwise by the parents (and particularly the mother) through treating (or not treating) the two children as a single individual. This observation seemed rooted on a maternal concern about doing just that and the presence of an observer seemed to help to scaffold the development of each individual infant in the mother's mind.

Bick (1964) cites how the birth of a child gives rise to changes in the patterns of identification of all members of the family; each must make a place for the newcomer in his mind—a specific place which was not occupied by anyone before. This clearly takes a certain time and the difficulty of the task is doubled with the arrival of twins. Liz was understandably overwhelmed by both the thought of and the arrival of "the girls" and lacked confidence in her own competence. Aided and abetted by David she seemed to appropriate one infant for herself, leaving the other to him, a solution which seemed to lend itself to further twinning scenarios between the parents.

As time went by Liz's confidence in her own good enough mothering increased and each twin was able to find their own space with her, their father and one another. Whilst Katie seemed much more independent and separate than her sister, Jo was able to meet with her mother in a more regressive relationship, to communicate her needs and to find adaptations to meet them. This observation clearly played an important and valuable part in facilitating this process and supporting Katie and Jo's unique journeys toward separation and individuation.

References

Athanassiou, C. (1986). A study of the vicissitudes of identification in twins. *International Journal of Psychoanalysis, 67*: 329–335.

Bick, E. (1964). Notes on infant observation in psychoanalytic training. *International Journal Psychoanalysis, 45*: 558–566.

Burlingham, D. (1952). *Twins: A Study of Three Pairs of Identical Twins.* New York: International Universities Press.

Davison, S. (1992). Mother, other, self—love & rivalry for twins in their first year of life. *International Review of Psychoanalysis. 19*: 359–374.

Dibble, E. D. & Cohen, D. J. (1981). Personality development in identical twins. *Psychoanalytic Study of the Child, 36*: 45–70.

Freud, A. & Dann, S. (1951). An experiment in group upbringing. *Psychoanalytic Study of the Child, 6*: 127–168.

Leonard, M. J. (1961). Problems in identification and ego development in twins. *Psychoanalytic Study of the Child,* 16: 300–320.

Mahler, M. (1952). On child psychosis and schizophrenia: autistic and symbiotic psychoses. *Psychoanalytic Study of the Child, 7*: 286–305.

Orr, D. W. (1941). A psychoanalytic study of a fraternal twin. *Psychoanalytic Quarterly, 10*: 284–296.

Piontelli, A. (1989). A study on twins before and after birth. *International Review of Psychoanalysis, 16*: 413–426.

Stern, D. N. (1985). *The Interpersonal World of the Human Infant.* New York: Basic Books.

Notes

1. From The Quotations Page (www.quotationspage.com).
2. Ibid.

CHAPTER TWO

Tsunami Boy

Ellie Roberts

The subject of my paper is the attempt to explore the impact of the internal twin on the transference during the therapy of a five-year-old boy.

Recently our attention has been drawn to the importance of sibling relationships and how they may have been overlooked, in the psychoanalytic field, especially with reference to the transference and in their importance for a child's emotional and social development. Juliet Mitchell (2003) in her book on *Siblings* sees psychoanalysts as favouring vertical relationships interpreting the maternal and paternal transference above that of the sibling transference. Mitchell (2003) writes that sibling relationships are not only important for social structures (pp. 1–4) but the presence of an internalized siblings relationship (p. 35) is fundamental to working out our future love choices and adult bonds. In psychoanalytic work, the consideration of the therapist as a sibling in the transference can help the working out of competitiveness, rivalry, envy, and aggression, along with more positive feelings of companionship. As we know from observational studies of the young child the birth of a younger sibling more often than not produces tumultuous feelings in the toddler. As Winnicott (1965) said with the birth of a sibling is "the loss of something that was good, and I am intending to imply that something happened, after which nothing was the same again" (p. 50).

When the sibling is a twin and the relationship begins in utero the processes of individuation are more complex. Harris Williams (1998) imaginatively evokes, using the wisdom of the poets, the sensory experience of intrauterine life before what she calls the "shipwreck" of birth. In this world the placenta is the other, a soft responsive friend where the rhythms of heartbeat and syncopation of the noises of the intrauterine environment provide the first experience of otherness. How much more for the twin, then another heartbeat, a whole other world, an intimate knowing, at one and the same time competitive and companionable. This imaginative account is borne out by Piontelli's (1992) observation of twins using ultrasound. She observes that the individual differences between these cohabitees ranged from the conditions of the environment they occupied, space, fluid, noise, and relationship to the placenta but also in the variation in response to the other twin. Some twins were observed to make contact but actively withdrew, whilst others "could be gentle, with the twins engaged in an mutual and seemingly affectionate cheek to cheek stroking" (p. 112). These modes of behaviour observed in utero were thought by Piontelli to continue into post uterine life. Later she refined this idea suggesting that this early experience was sensate rather than cognitive, therefore, leaving an indistinct memory rather than a discreet one.

Bion (1967) came to regard the idea of psychological twinning as less important, returning to a more Kleinian view of it as a variant of splitting processes. However, in his paper on the "Imaginary Twin" he had considered three patients, all of whom held phantasies about a twin, either taken from reality or imaginary. In Patient A, the imaginary twin is not allowed to be born, and anxiety is kept at bay in this way. Psychically the imaginary twin disallows the patient freedom and independence. What is the meaning of an imaginary twin? Bion says that with Patient A "that the imaginary twin goes back to his earliest relationship and is an expression of his inability to tolerate an object that was not entirely under his control" (p. 19). The function of the imaginary twin was thus to deny a reality different from himself. In the course of the analytic work the analyst is experienced as the unborn twin potentially disallowing the patient's freedom. Bion describes how there has to be a fundamental shift through the analytic work from the two "I" s to a "you" and a "me". When this shift has been achieved oedipal material can emerge and be worked through in the transference. Up until then the analyst is experienced in the transference as the imaginary twin. Lewin (2004) explores in great detail the nature of the twin transference and highlights the way in which these patients attempt to create a twin relationship with the analyst, the existence of a narcissistic relating to the analyst that denies the existence of the other as separate and works against change towards individuality.

In my case example Sam has to recover from a catastrophe, that of the psychic loss of his twin in utero, through an experience akin to a tsunami where he emerges pulled out by the obstetrician's rubber gloves covered in a cowl of dead skin that deadens him. In phantasy his sister is dead and even the concrete reality of a live, able, sister does not cure this. He seems unable to mourn, he struggles with occupying a female identity, he attempts to fuse with the lost object, he becomes excited in a fetishistic way trying, it seems, to reach a lost nirvana, and revels in nostalgia. At times his loneliness is palpable and for a time he turned to God, Jesus, and the resurrection as way of securing an everlasting companion but also saving him from the work he has to do.

Sam was five years old when he came into therapy. Many specialists had seen Sam. Was he autistic, dyspraxic, and deaf, brain damaged or suffering from some rare syndrome? Sam, apparently, was not able to make use of school, did not understand situations, could not speak in sentences, and seemed unable to control his body. According to his mother no one seemed to be able to make a diagnosis, let alone offer any help. The circumstances of his birth had been traumatic and yet this mother wrestled with the fact that the obstetrician had reassured her that although Sam was born by emergency Caesura with the cord around his neck, he had not lacked oxygen for a significant amount of time. Sam is a twin and the labour was induced at thirty-seven weeks because it was thought that Sam's sister was not growing and was small for dates. In fact, it was Sam that was small, lying high up and squashed in his mother's womb. His sister was born quickly vaginally and this created a vacuum and the pressure burst Sam's intrauterine waters and he became distressed. It was only in retrospect that I have been able to think about the way Sam entered the therapy.

The assessment was in late November and it was arranged that he would begin once a week therapy in the January. This gap between the assessment and the beginning of therapy was, in part, driven by my intuition that this mother was not entirely convinced about what she was embarking on and too much haste might have alarmed her and also because I was conscious that the break would come too quickly after the commencement of the therapy. These thoughts were redundant in many ways, as the break between the assessment and the first term seemed to be experienced by Sam dramatically and bled into his experience of the natural disaster on Boxing Day that year, the Tsunami.

The assessment session

"Getting in" seemed to be immediate. This beautiful boy fell into the consulting room, having given his mother a backwards look as she retreated up the drive. The symmetry of his features, the colour of his skin, his bright lively eyes seemed in contrast to the pain of watching him flail about wrestling with his coat and tripping over his shoelaces. He also seemed to be lalling, or was it scribble talk or was he singing, it was a production that seemed ongoing without an external audience. His clumsy body seemed quite separate from the ease with which he used the space and furniture. It was as if he had always been there in my room, he had merely encountered me as Keats (1964) says, "like a watcher of the skies. When a new planet swims into his ken" (on first looking into Chapman's Homer).

As he surveyed the small room, taking his time, he gave equal regard to the outside, looking through the window and a word emerging from the scribble talk arrived "The big house". The presence of the outside and the big house seemed to stimulate his interest in the inside of the consulting room. Turning to me he said questioningly, "Your bedroom?" "Where are the books?" "Have you a sister?"

We were in an intrauterine space and I was to have my role. Mostly I was to be questioned about my origins. I would have to be a repository of the answers to all the questions Sam would like to know about. Sam was not so much in the process of gathering the transference as establishing a profile of me as an object, born not out of the epistemophilic instinct, but more from the need to cover up the real tragedy, namely the loss of an object with which he had great intimacy, his sister/mother in utero. To Sam's questions I adopted an even tone, accepting equally what I understood and what I didn't. I was now given to believe that I was the bigger, knowing sister. All this was accompanied by the playing with the string he had found which became a "necklace around his neck" echoing the umbilical cord around his neck, and then a kite, with Sam in one corner of the room holding one end of the string and myself in my position holding the other. As he wound the string around his hand it brought him closer to me and he played this game over and over again. At that moment I seemed to be at the end of an umbilical cord, him pulling me in. He had demonstrated his interest in the space and me and I looked forward to beginning the work. He left knowing he would return in January.

His return in January to begin the therapy saw him hurtling down the drive but with a steady look in his eye finding my eyes and holding on to them. Each arrival during the term at the consulting room presented the problem of how to get out of his winter coat. Usually after some distracted attempts he would stick out one sleeve and request that I pull. The first few weeks he picked up the theme from the assessment, playing with the string, the tangle, and the connection with me, and the pleasure at discovering each week that the string was where he had left it. However, the material had a boredom intrinsic in it consonant with the deadening effects of control. It seems that the string game that inaugurated my relationship with him is his attempt at rehearsing the extent to which he is capable of being in control of the closeness that I tantalizingly offer him, similar to Freud's (1920) version of the "fort da" game (pp. 14–15). But the beginning and his encounter with me in the consulting room also seemed to fill Sam with anxiety about impending separations and death. Not only was he constantly worried about holidays that were months away, he was able to communicate something of his very first fears; we had the psychic circumstances of his birth in vivo. He tells me the problem "pop-a-teel". When I struggled to understand what he was saying he said it was Italian and then he said, "I can't speak Swedish and I can't speak Polish." I had in mind here the way in which coming from a bilingual family created a dimension that baffled him and excluded him especially as he did not know his mother tongue. Always two languages with one unknown. I talked of how he did not understand and how he was coming to see a Mrs Roberts to think about these things and he said, "What will you do with me in the summer? I'm going to Sweden. Will you go to Sweden? I won't be in Peking or Russia, will you? Do you speak Russian? I don't understand Swedish. It is snowing in Val d'Isere. I want to stay here for a long time. I'm going to tell my Mum I want to stay for a long time." I said that perhaps coming here could be like the long piece of string, there was no rush. He began to cut little bits off the string. He lost me over the next few minutes, as his speech disappeared into scribble. He said, "I'll meet you next summer. Do you have a telephone number?" I talked of his worries that he's not sure that he'll be able to find me and he, therefore, believes that I'll not be able to find him. He said, sitting on the couch and looking at me and then away from me, "I'm going to die. I am going to get old and die." He began to scribble talk again and said something like "treance" and pointing at the picture on the wall he said, "I'd like to make a picture using skin, make a picture out of skin." I was struggling to make sense of his words when I realised the word he was trying to say was "tsunami". I said that he seemed to be thinking about the people that died in the tsunami wave. He said, "Yes, they were probably wearing white gloves. Those babies floated in the waves and then they died. It's so sad, it's just so sad. I'm going to stop that wave, I'm going to brush it away and I'm going to get the sun out till it gets hot. The babies had the dead skin."

Imaginatively I felt that this was Sam's story, the story of his birth from which he had at some point and for some time retreated, as if he couldn't come alive psychically. He was born from the vacuum created by something he seemed to perceive as a loss. There was no stopping the story of the tsunami and for a few weeks Sam came with the story of the "island", "a whoosh of water, deep water". Lying on the couch with his thumb in his mouth, "So sad. Saw it in Italy, people dead, frightened." When I began to interpret his own worries about something whooshing, something gone, something rushing, he said to me "When I was born, Lucy was born. When you were born, I was second. "Lucy won." Why have you got two cushions? Did you want a twin? How long does it take to get born? Three minutes, feel it was a 100 minutes."

The problem of "two" seemed to mean that Sam had cancelled himself out. If one is born does it mean the other is dead? What's the problem with two? It certainly had created many questions in Sam's mind. Here it seems that whatever his capacity for reality testing regarding his sister, in psychic reality this twin-in-utero sister was irretrievably lost. Was it that this sister perhaps had given him the experience of a skin while he remained unborn? The pain of the work of relating to Sam lies in this quality of him being unborn occupying dead skin, a catastrophe from which he has to recover. Esther Bick's (1987) understanding was that "until the containing functions of the object have been introjected the concept of space within the self cannot arise" and that prior to that the self is held together by the skin functioning as a boundary and that faulty development of this primal skin impairs introjective processes, leading to the development of a second-skin formation which later produces a "general fragility in later integration and organizations" (p. 114). It seems that in order to recover from the catastrophe and the dead skin/object responsible for a dead/deadening part of himself he would have to embark on a process of mourning and reality testing.

During the work, the room as the intrauterine place was eagerly sought. Sam would act out "bedtime" using the couch where he would seek comfort in his sister's bed. This was represented by Sam as crawling into his sister's bed and "getting boiling". The two of them are shown getting dressed and his fear that the whole thing would be cleared away, "Oh I do hope Olga does not come and do the cleaning." His desire to climb into bed and get hot and exciting with his sister, fulfilling his desired fusion seemed to be ways of defending himself against the more painful psychic realities of his loss. Here in the room he was happy to be in my bed/couch far away from the demands of the day.

However, the work moved on and I was in pain but I did not know it until one day when it was my turn to present in a small supervision group and I felt a very urgent, emotional need to talk of this boy. I was at sea, and his need to find a location resonated in me as I struggled also to come to terms with bearing the pain and beauty of what had been glimpsed and lost. When I was with Sam there were moments when he could captivate me, his emotional response to the beauty of the world would leave me feeling an acute and fundamental loss that did not leave me feeling empty. Maybe I can convey some of this to you.

Sam arrived and going straight to the window, talking as if we had been talking all morning he quietly said, "Its snowing, lovely snow." He immediately took up a position near the window to watch the snowflakes. He turned around to find me in my chair and he came across to me and presented himself, anorak still zipped up to his chin. After some conversation about the Easter holidays that were by now still a month away he said, "In Brenov it rains." I said that he had two places in his mind. He said, "In England there are owls and foxes." His voice trailed off and in its place I had a visual emotional experience of the beauty of this place, and of his understanding, his knowledge, a boy with so many questions but also who knew too much, too early. By the last weeks before the Easter break we had worked and reworked his worries and some new material emerged, that of his noticing his bisexuality. This manifested itself in several ways, the manufacture of feminine objects. "A pretty necklace" his plaintiff request for beads, "Oh I wish I had beads.". His pull towards sensuality often emerged in the sessions. His desire to stroke my tights, his enjoyment in flopping down on the couch and twiddling some piece of fabric. Eventually Sam as a boy seemed more secure. however, the excitement of the "white gloves" developed into what he called the nappy game. "I like the white gloves" he said, leaving me perplexed but also remembering this image in the tsunami material, and my conjecture of the obstetrician lifting him out of his own tsunami. After much confusion, the story emerged of the baby on the changing mat. He flopped down on the couch to demonstrate his knees held up to his tummy and his bottom in the air and the white gloves above him. Here he was the "bottom baby". He interrupted his excitement himself when sitting up breathless from his enactment he said looking at me "I was born in mummy's tummy, where were you born?"

His excitement in the room often threatened the work as I had to be the one having a nappy and he stuffed paper towels into my lap and finding a red felt tip pen I was also to have a "willy". When I interpreted his desire for me to be the boy baby that could be a throwaway bottom baby and that only boys had willies he protested and said that everyone has a willy. Eventually, now resorting to his lalling and singing he said thoughtfully to me and sheepishly "girls no willy" and when I reflected this back to him he said that their willies had been chopped off. The idea that this alarming experience of birth had produced a sewage baby was explained by Sam. Sitting on the chair, his legs swinging and twiddling with the string he said, "I do not really like gloves now because I am grown up. I am going to clean up that sea, those people died because the sewage had got into the sea, pooh had floated around and got into their throats. I'll clean the sea, I'll get crabs, lots of crabs and animals, lots of snails and fish, I'll give people food and the water would be very clear and I'll grow up and get a sail boat and I'll go to the island and clean it all up. Perhaps God will help. Where is God? Do you know? I know he has a big drum and that he could help with that tsunami." In response to my link with his own internal landscape he said, "I don't like deep water, it's frightening. When you are a baby you do not know whether it is deep or shallow." And then thoughtfully he said, "Resting on your special bed, so sad, that tsunami so sad, saw it in Italy, saw the wave." Sam's omnipotence in saving the babies from drowning in their own faeces filled my mind with the enormity of the tragedy he had to defend against. Often I felt like a bystander listening to a monologue in a Beckett play – there was a world that he inhabited that was exclusive to him. His questioning did not really demand a desire to know me but a camouflage of the real problem.

Bion (1987) describes the caesura. He is using the image of a Picasso painting on glass so that the image can be seen on both sides. He said "the same thing can be said of the caesura, it depends which way you look at it, which way you are travelling" (p. 306). The penetration of thought and experience across the caesura both ways seems to have been available to Sam.

The first holiday break at Easter finally came and on his return I noticed a change in that he began to become interested in me directly. I seemed to have progressed from an intrauterine companion/competitor to a tentative someone. He came after the Easter break sadly telling me, "I did not have any dreams about you. I did have a dream about the sea." Then looking closely at me he leant forward to touch my scarf that I had bought in the Easter holidays in Sicily. "How did you get this scarf? Was it made by artists?" Then stroking the cushion on the couch he said, "Do you think artists made this too? It takes a lot of work to make a cushion. I really missed you." When in response to some further material, I interpreted his loneliness he said, "How did you know I'd come?" With an awareness of my presence and absence came an interest in the others that I saw. Looking out of the window, "Do you feed the birds? Do they get breakfast and lunch and supper?"

Variations on this theme punctuated the term's sessions. However, his interest in my permanence came by his experimenting with many games involving a cushion. Holding the cushion in front of his face and mine he'd experiment with a peek-a-boo type of game, which seemed to be about whether I went on existing when he could not see me and also reflected that twoness separated by the intrauterine membrane. This theme was followed up the week later when he began to draw. "I'm going to draw daddy," but the daddy became a baby daddy and then got mixed up with a mummy. He talked of growing and tried to make the figures grown up simply by making their legs longer. I was aware of his dawning sense of some differential between me and him, his new knowledge of this thing called "grown up" but I said to him that there was no rush, he had time. The absence of any oedipal material had often made the sessions dull and repetitive. It was as if there was no room, no need for parents, the twins, that is he and I, were self-sufficient. He then said, "Why are you called Mrs. Roberts?" I said that was because there was a Mr Roberts. He asked, "Is he your baby?" I interpreted his denial of a grown up mummy and daddy that look after the babies. He said, "Have you had a baby in your tummy last year?" and then to my surprise "Was your daddy running in the race?" I had forgotten about actually seeing Sam in the park at the weekend. He then said, "I did not speak to you because I did not know you would be at the Park." I commented that when he is not thinking about me, it is as if I am nowhere. He smiled and said, "You were walking away and looked very busy" and he imitated my walk and I said, "In your mind I was a mummy thinking about a daddy, we did not say hello but remember we smiled at each other." He said, "Will you go to the park next Sunday?"

As the work progressed, I became aware of never really hearing about Sam's family or his outside world, let alone his twin sister. The sense was of the therapy being in a bubble, a bubble that I had been co-opted into, to do what I wasn't sure. Both of us, that is as "me" and "him", "therapist" and "patient", "woman" and "child" had not yet been born. There seemed to be not only a denial of external realities but also his inability to tolerate internal psychic realities. Suddenly there seemed to me to be less time and an urgency.

In the following October, during a review with Sam's mother, I heard about how well Sam was doing. School were very pleased with him. His speech and language were really developing, he was beginning to learn, and he was less clumsy. He was doing well. As the work progresses Sam has shown me some of the problems of achieving a "you and me." Sam engages me in playing games. He has just celebrated his seventh birthday. He engages me in playing games but the games cannot work. I am to guess what in the room has been removed and hidden in the waiting room, or to guess what is missing from a box of toys he has selected without having seen the selection before, or he lets me see him hiding his coat and then asks me what is missing. Is it that our minds are the same so I will know? It is clear something is hiding, missing, lost, but there is only half the story to go on, everything is half understood. Only understanding half gave way to a confessed hate of his twin sister and the half that she had, that is the feminine half. Sam began to make "willies" and wrap them up in paper, they were presents for me that were to be opened at night, we were to be the same. Eventually he tells me that he wishes his twin sister was a boy and then they would be the same. Sam asks, "If she hasn't got a willy, what has she got inside?" However, he seems to know something of this when he then says to me, "I'm going to sleep in your house and drink your juice." Back in the room I am to find the thing that is missing. I say, "You want me to know where the missing thing is?" He says, "Inside Greta, lost my mind." He is playing with the dough, "This is your womb, open it up and the baby comes out. You can see the baby. You can see the twin. How long ago was I in mummy's tummy?" These moments cannot be sustained and give way to a nostalgia, a place before time began. The longing for nursery and the room becomes infused with an ideal time and now seems lost. "Rubber gloves, the nappy game, blow them, pull them, I like blowing them. They were all nice, all left. Julia, Maria, Sylvia, they all had babies. Such a lovely time in nursery. I loved Cheryl. Every day at nursery get a story. Donna has gone. I loved gloves. You had lunch, went in the sand pit. They lived upstairs in the nursery and then they've gone."

How can he shake off this dead sister's skin to come alive as himself? The process seems to be one of projective identification into the dead internal object, the start of which cannot be pinpointed in time but we may speculate that it began in the comings and goings of intrauterine life and set in motion at the point of separation through the birth of these two babies. I have suggested that Sam's development was being curtailed by defensive structures put in place to defend against catastrophic anxieties. Meltzer (1973) has explored the nature of some forms of psychic pain; in particular: terror, persecution, and dread. Is it that Sam experienced the immediacy of the loss of his sister, inducing in him guilt leading to an immediate projective identification into what was to become the dead baby object? Meltzer's (1973) patient dreams of dead babies, octopuses, worms, and crabs and the consequent terror suffered by the patient that he has destructively attacked the internal babies. Meltzer says that in his patient it is terror of the dead babies and his destructiveness that leads to a narcissistic defensive structure. Sam struggles to make sense in the room. Are these communications what Bion (1992) calls Beta Elements, "undigested" and "undreamed facts" (p. 64) that have not been transformed by the alpha function that makes up containment? Certainly this is not symbolic thinking and the depressive position is not achieved. However, my experience as the receiver of the communications was that these were Sam's efforts at communicating thoughts not yet able to be thought. How can he tear himself away from the symmetry and seductive nostalgia of the intrauterine nirvana? How can he face the nameless dread consequent to his loss and the persecutory anxiety of drowning in his own faeces? He needs to begin the oedipal journey and come alive to the world of others. However, the capacity for sadness about the tsunami, coming from a different part of himself, provides some hope of his potential to relate and to learn from experience.

In this paper I have described the work with Sam and his struggle to make contact with the therapist and emerge from the limited world of twinship, from the psychic retreat of a nirvana state on the one hand and nameless dread on the other.

I would like to thank Alberto Hahn and the members of the small supervision group that I belong to, Andrea Watson, Irene Freeden, Jacqui Ferguson, and Denise Cullington for their ideas and thoughtfulness about my work.

References

Bion, W. (1967). *Second Thoughts*. London: Maresfield.

Bion, W. (1989). *Caesura*. London: Karnac Books.

Bion, W. (1992). *Cogitations*. London: Karnac Books.

Harris Williams, M. (1998). The ugly duckling. *The Journal Of Melanie Klein and Object Relations, 16:* 2.

Keats. (Ed.) Roger Sharrock (1964). *New Oxford English Series*. Oxford University Press.

Lewin, V. (2004). *The Twin in the Transference*. London: Whurr.

Meltzer, D. (1973). *Sexual States of Mind*. London: The Clunie Press.

Mitchell, J. (2003). *Siblings: Sex & Violence*. Cambridge: Polity Press.

Piontelli, A. (1992). *From Fetus to Child*. London: Routledge.

Winnicott, D. (1965). *The Family and Individual Development*. London: Tavistock.

CHAPTER THREE

The influence of conjoined twins on each other

Jeanne Magagna and Gloria Dominguez
with contribution by Alessandra Marsoni

Introduction

In 2004, Vivienne Lewin wrote: "Nothing appears to have been written in the psychoanalytic literature about the psychological consequences of being a conjoined twin or the surgical separation of the twins" (Lewin, 2004, p. 178). This chapter describes a psychoanalytic, observational study of the relationship between conjoined twins, Tom and Peter, during 18 months of hospitalization, both before and after they were separated. This study highlights the intense attachment and closeness between conjoined twins and shows how the absence or presence of certain personal and constitutional characteristics have a crucial impact on the way identical external traumas of separation and loss are endured. The concepts of splitting and projective identification are also illustrated; for example, we see how personality growth in Peter is enhanced by his ability to face and struggle with a conflictual situation and respond to it in an *active way that can be noticed* by the caregivers in hospital. On the other hand, Tom lived in identification with his more active sibling's cry for help and he existed in identification with Peter's assertiveness for food and people's company. This fostered slowness and weakness in the development of Tom's more passive personality. In addition, we explore how the conjoined twins, Tom and Peter, develop and use attachments to each other and to the caregivers to work through their pain linked with multiple surgical interventions and their multiple losses. These losses include the loss of an attached body that is experienced as integral to each twin's sense of being; the loss of each other in terms of the intense closeness of the other twin; and the repeated losses of either mother or father as they travelled to and from the rest of the family in Portugal. This conjoined twin study shows how very early the capacity for empathy can develop in young babies, particularly in conjoined twins. Since the conjoined twins developed from one ovum and shared the same womb, it is interesting to note how nature and nurture impact on one another as the twins develop.

A crisis can either be a stimulus for growth of the personality or the force determining psychological regression. Perhaps the inherent personality characteristics of the infant partially determine which path—growth or regression—the infant takes. Having a twin conjoined to one's body, sharing similar physical and sometimes emotional experiences, leads to the possibility of internalizing a strong bond to the other twin. There is a great psychological and physical danger in being passively reliant on the other twin as an attachment figure. This passive dependence on the other conjoined twin can lead to a retreat from frustrations of emotional dependence on the parents and hospital caregivers. A normal development of the tie to the parents is essential for healthy development of the personality. The mother constitutes the facilitating environment making the steady progress of the maturational process possible (Winnicott, 1960) and laying the basic foundation for the baby's secure attachment. From this develops a sense of trust in a responsive environment. The presence of a healthy, sociable conjoined twin alongside a more fragile, passive twin can obscure the emotional passivity and concomitant social deprivation for both twins.

Peter and Tom were eight-month-old Portuguese conjoined twins brought to a paediatric hospital in order to be surgically separated.

Participant observation

The observations of the conjoined twins, Peter and Tom, were undertaken on a weekly basis by Gloria Dominquez who had already completed a course of infant observation as outlined in *Intimate Transformations: Babies with their Families* (Magagna et al., 2005). Jeanne Magagna, Consultant Child Psychotherapist in the hospital where the twins resided, supervised Gloria Dominquez' observations. At a certain point Gloria was encouraged to be involved in *participant observing* which is described below.

The observations consisted of weekly, hour-long visits, according to the method of Mrs. Esther Bick (1968) that stresses using the emotional responses of the observer as a crucial part of the observational task. During the twins' stay in hospital, mother and father alternately visited the hospital and then left the twins for weeks at a time to return to their other four children in Portugal. For this reason participant observations were felt to be essential in facilitating some understanding in nursing staff and continuity for the twins. The participant observations involved voicing to the parents and/or nurses the observations made about the twins and their relationships. The primary task was to facilitate the caregivers' understanding of the differing individual needs of each infant. The observer also created a dialogue with the parents and nurses in order to enable the caregivers to deepen their understanding of the differing emotional experiences of the twins through making their own more detailed observations of the conjoined twins' interactions within the network of nurses, doctors and the conjoined twins.

It was essential for the observer to enable the conjoined twins to be differentiated as having separate voices, separate personality characteristics and separate spaces in the minds of their caretakers. It was also important to see how deeply they were connected to each other, not only physically, but also emotionally. Through the participant observation, both the parents and the primary nurses were enabled to develop more intimate relationships with the twins. The parents also gained more confidence in relating to their twins. The nurses had a multitude of physical caregiving tasks, that initially they alone performed for the twins. Because there was so much international publicity given to the fact that these were conjoined twins, there was a tendency for both nurses and parents to offer the twins shared rather than individuated experiences. For this reason it was crucial that the observer enable the parents to develop their parental roles more specifically for each child. The participant observer did this by trying to spend one half of each observational hour seeing the world through the eyes of one twin by observing and commenting on one twin's activity and relationships, and then she would focus on the other twin's experiences. The observer's intent was to enable the caregivers to modify their responses to meet the distinct, unique needs of each twin while also thinking about the twins shared experiences and dependence on each other's capacities and fragilities.

During the 21 months the twins remained in hospital in order to be surgically separated and have their separated bodies repaired, there were so many physical interventions requiring nurse and doctor's interventions and medical equipment that the parents could easily feel left out of ordinary parenting tasks. For this reason the nurses were encouraged to help and support the parents gradually learn to undertake more necessary medical roles for the children. There was also a crucial need for the observer to foster the rescue of the passive twin, Tom who tended to rely too much on both the assertiveness of his brother, Peter, who took almost all the initiatives in feeding and playing and relating to people.

A brief description of the twins and the nature of conjoined twinning

Peter and Tom are the product of a single ovum. They are monozygotic twins, having the same sex and similar palmar and epidermal characteristics. Conjoined twinning is thought to result from the imperfect division of the embryo after the formation of two embryonic discs (Bryan, 1993). The development of the division of the embryo is stopped or retarded at a critical period of susceptibility, thereby inducing abnormal budding or fusion of the embryonic disc. Another explanation to account for the incompletely divided embryonic disc is the initiation of two or more areas of axial growth. The critical period of susceptibility is soon after the formation of the rudimentary amniotic sac in the blastula stage, when there is a two-layered embryo four or five days after the ovum is fertilized.

At the time of writing this paper there are approximately 300 sets of conjoined twins who have survived more than a few hours after birth.

Peter and Tom were described as thoracopagus conjoined twins because they were joined at the chest and the pelvis while sharing the same liver and the same intestinal tract. Tom and Peter also had some malformations not associated with being thoracopagus twins. The twin pair had two heads and two upper trunks, and Peter and Tom each had their own hearts and their own hands and arms. They thus appeared normal on the top half of their bodies. However, their lower trunk was a shared trunk, with a shared imperforated anus and shared penis. Peter had a left leg, and Tom a right leg. Their malformations might have been due to a lack of blood circulation or some other failure during the embryogenesis.

The Parents

Mother was a lively, talkative religious woman, in her late twenties, who kept links with her extended family while she normally devoted herself full time to the care of her children. She was very skilful and competent in many ways. Father, in his early thirties, was a plumber, who, because he worked long hours, had originally left much of the child rearing to his wife. As a consequence of the birth of conjoined twins requiring hospitalization in another country, he developed and enjoyed his caregiving role as a father to each twin. The couple already had four children who were physically normal.

At the time of giving birth, mother was not aware she was expecting conjoined twins. She was only told three days after their birth, as both she and they were in a delicate physical condition following the Caesarian delivery. For the same reasons she was also not allowed to see her children until they were 10 days old. They were in critical health and wired up to many medical devices to keep them alive in the intensive care unit. The doctors had never allowed breast-feeding because the babies required very sensitive and minimal handling.

The children's physical malformations seemed to be accepted by the parents with resignation and aplomb. Perhaps the extensive presence of international press and television publicity had influenced the parents to feel rather proud of giving birth to conjoined twins. However, mother was always firmly convinced that the twins should be separated and deep down she was relieved when this successfully occurred. Later she mentioned that some of her neighbours considered conjoined twins to be monsters. She refused the notion that surgery could be done to enable one child to have a more complete body at the expense of the other child. Determinedly she said, "Both children must stay alive". At a great sacrifice to their four other children and to father's work life, either mother or father travelled back to Portugal every three weeks while the other parent remained in the hospital with the twins.

Peter

Peter and Tom looked very alike with their attractive round faces, blond hair, green eyes and very long eyelashes; however, they could be easily differentiated by their muscular movements and personalities. Peter was pale, sickly looking and skinny. He moved his arms and leg frenetically as though he was easily agitated and almost always in distress. In fact, Peter often cried plaintively. Peter also had a penetrating gaze. At times his frowning facial expression looked like that of a wizened old man. He seemed mentally alert and very attentive to people and his surroundings. When he concentrated on a task, such as reaching for an object, he frowned and generally seemed to be thoughtful and inquisitive. Peter, the more active child, was initially the smaller of the two boys. The doctors thought that the boys' joined digestive systems functioned in such a way that Peter ate the food while, paradoxically, Tom gained the weight.

Tom

In contrast to Peter's searching gaze, Tom had a more receptive gaze. He engaged people in such a way that he was continually described as sweet and as "a good boy". He didn't cry as frequently as Peter. He was more accepting of the way things were, not making much fuss when he was distressed and not making many demands for social interaction. While he enjoyed father's playing with him, he often seemed to be willing to be placated by looking at a colourful toy or receiving a dummy into his mouth.

The experience of "two as one"

Tom and Peter, aged eight months, arrived in the hospital for their surgical separation. Their parents accompanied them and father described how proud he was to have conjoined twins. Father was keen to show his expert knowledge of the twins' differences in anatomy and the ways their bodies functioned. He also went into great detail about the twins' differing behaviour and sizes. Surprisingly father showed no obvious anxiety regarding the attendant risk that both or one of the twins might die through the medical interventions to separate their bodies.

The birth of the twins had brought neither one nor two babies. Instead it brought a confusing situation. Were they one or two, as they shared the same lower half of their bodies? The situation of malformed babies joined together was too overwhelming and confusing for the parents. These feelings prompted the parents towards developing a closer relationship with Tom, the heavier, bigger, less complaining baby. It seemed that the parents unconsciously chose Tom because he seemed healthier and more appreciative of their parental efforts to look after him. After the boys were surgically separated at 21 months, Peter, who now had his own distinctive digestive system and had been used to regularly seeking and taking in more nourishment, gradually became the healthier looking, more energetic, more demanding, more sociable, and more obviously capable twin. At this point the parents' unconscious preference for a closer relationship with Tom changed and they seemed more attentive to Peter.

Various observations of the parents' behaviour supported the idea of their finding it possible to relate intimately to only one of the conjoined twins. The parents almost continually attempted to make the twins do the same things, or play with the same toy. More specifically, the parents persistently wanted Tom to play with whatever toy Peter was handling. This tendency to make the twins "two as one", and the same, indicated how difficult it was for the parents to bear the emotional and physical burden of having two separate human beings, who might have both similar and different sets of emotional needs. Tom was less capable than Peter, or at least appeared to be unwilling to make the same effort as Peter. Tom often joined Peter in play and then couldn't keep up, and retreated into himself or started crying in frustration. His cries were interpreted by the parents as meaning that Tom was tired or physically unwell. It was difficult for the parents to imagine that he often felt inadequate, left out and not attuned to the expectation that he was to have the identical competence and alacrity as Peter in all activities such as grabbing a ball, putting it into his mouth, and handing it back to the parents.

Being "two as one" was in part a physical fact for the twins who initially shared the same lower digestive tract. However, they continued to be regarded as "two as one" in the caregiver's minds beyond what was necessary or helpful. As an example of "two as one", Peter, the more active, resourceful twin elicited simultaneous caregiving for both boys when he cried and ate food from which Tom benefitted. However, while Peter was eating for both Tom and himself, they were actually two separate individuals as regards personality and emotionality, and each needed to be treated according to his specific needs.

Rivalry between the boys was muted, but it became more apparent when an adult offered them a toy. It may also be that the twins had not introjected sufficiently good individual care-giving on a regular basis to give them the inner strength to bear the conflict involved in competing with each other, while at the same time sharing a lower body and consequently not being able to retreat from one another. Even in that situation, however, the boys often seemed to adapt to each other by finding a way of mutually enjoying the same toy rather than fighting over toys. At times it seemed that their physical connectedness influenced the transformation of their competition for a toy, to co-operation in sharing the same toy. We wondered if the two boys frequently experienced themselves in a *symbiotic union,* perhaps feeling themselves to be one person. It was noticeable that neither twin glanced at the other's face, nor did they touch the other, even when encouraged by mother. Usually the boys did not do the same thing until a caregiver approached them. The presence of a third person, an adult, precipitated a tendency in the twins to move towards focusing on the same object or reaching for it. The following excerpt exemplifies this.

Twins: 10 months old

> Tom and Peter are happy trying to catch single toys that are simultaneously being placed in front of them. At one moment there is a very mild competition as they each try to grab the same little brown toy

> puppy that has been presented. The competition ends as each boy grasps a different ear of the toy puppy and simultaneously and co-operatively each sucks on a separate ear. They seemed to enjoy doing the same thing with the same object simultaneously.

At times like this, the children's play suggested a mirror-like relationship. When one did something, the other one followed suit. It was often difficult to notice a defined initiator of the play sequence. Sometimes it was obvious that Tom was copying Peter's behaviour or wanting to play with the same toy Peter had. At another time, Tom, the more passive twin, took the initiative to hit Peter with a little toy car. The only response Peter made to being approached and hit by Tom was to close his eyes. On one occasion when Tom, most unusually, began to babble to beckon the nurses, Peter attempted to sit up. It was, of course, an impossible feat for Peter to sit up unless Tom also sat up, as their abdomens were joined as one.

The conjoined twins, being "two in one body" faced the difficulties and pleasures of having to endure together in a twinship, through 24-hour cycles of play, feeding, and sleeping. The perpetual union of their bodies enabled the twins to rely on the actual physical presence of each other and become very attached to one another as they coped with the major upheaval of one or another parent going to Portugal to look after the four children there. Occasionally for a few days neither parent was with the twins in hospital.

Separating the twins

Surgical separation of the twins took place when they were 10 ½ months. The day-long surgery was followed by medication that kept the boys unconscious or virtually asleep for almost a month. The doctors used this medication because they were concerned that if the boys were fully conscious during this time they would move about too much, be in too much pain and would jeopardize the healing of their wounds and repairs. Each boy had differing life-threatening physical complications following the surgery and, therefore, Peter and Tom were kept apart in different specialist medical wards for several months. They did, however, have some playtime together when they awakened. This shared time was ostensibly arranged in order to make visiting the boys less arduous for the parents. The observer felt that the boys had suffered being apart in rooms separate from one another, when they were so obviously so attached to one another.

When separated and fully clothed both Peter and Tom looked normal other than each missing one leg. However, underneath their clothing each boy had an external colostomy plastic bag to collect the faeces extracted from their bowels. They also had "peg feeding", involving a tube attached to their stomach. Now each boy had a stomach, an anus and a newly constructed penis.

The observation below indicates the extent to which Tom was traumatized by the separation.

Tom: eleven months, two weeks

> A day after Tom awakened from the month long medicated sleep, mother held a mirror in front of him. Tom looked into the mirror and frowned. Then he began to whine in obvious terror and distress. Mother said, "Tom". She pointed at his head whilst holding the mirror before him. Tom refused to look at the mirror, looking instead at his mother's face, which she placed before the mirror. Then he calmed down.

It was tortuous to watch mother present the mirror to Tom. He clearly wanted to cling onto his mother's face. It was mother who was needed as a mirror for the twins to understand their new emotional and physical experiences. It was mother who was needed to support Peter and Tom with their sense of loss of each other. It was mother who was needed to support Tom's loss of his sociable and thoughtful self-located in Peter. It was mother and father who were needed to help each boy, but particularly Tom, with the anxieties of being a baby physically different, separate from a lifelong companion to whom he had been previously physically joined both inside and outside the womb for 17 and one-half months. The trauma of a new separate existence in which each boy had to eat and evoke the caregiver's presence through crying was particularly difficult for Tom. For it was Tom who had been using Peter as a primary object. Tom was particularly dependent on Peter's living for two. It was at the point of separation from his brother that Tom became increasingly passive, depressed and isolated.

Separation and loss of identity

Having been born prematurely, Tom and Peter were young for their 10½ months of age. Because they were so young, no one knew how to properly prepare them for the fact that when they awakened to consciousness, they would be split apart from one another. Each twin missed a leg, but more importantly they were missing each other. They were no longer a part of one another, dependant on each other's presence, on their shared trunk and legs, on their emotional attachment to each other as primary presences. They had introjected the experience of being joined as one. Now each was a different person from before. Each was a separate, unique person, able to sleep in a different bed or even a different room from the other. Their deep sense of loss of a lifelong ever-present companion was apparent. The fact that they were no longer able to depend on one another was a very demanding emotional realization. They had to face sudden new responsibilities for their own physical and emotional survival.

The twins were literally cut in half from the trunk downwards and one wonders if the experience of being two felt like being cut in half psychologically with parts of the self located in the other twin. This thought arose in observing a particular game that father and mother frequently played during the three months subsequent to the boys' surgical separation.

Peter and Tom: 13 months

> Father lifted Peter in the air in front of Tom, who was lying down in bed. As Tom saw Peter lifted above him, he screamed, shook his head as if repelling something noxious and then turned his head away from the scene. There was a distinct impression that Tom was being tortured by the separation from Peter.

The parents also played the same game lifting Tom in the air while Peter lay on the bed. It elicited a similarly distressed response in Peter. We wondered why the parents repeatedly played this game. The boys' perilous, lengthy operation had been a success. The international press, the doctors and nurses, the hospital staff, and particularly the parents were celebrating a triumph. Both of the conjoined twins had stayed alive! The parents' game of throwing each twin in the air separately was part of a celebration of having two "normal" babies.

However, both Tom and Peter could not bear to look at each other for several months after the operation. They found the separation frightening and difficult, as if they had lost a part of themselves. We were reminded of some other conjoined twins who, when separated at aged three, had each reassigned their own name to the other. This name exchange seemed connected to the traumatic loss of each other. Perhaps because of the celebratory atmosphere around the successful separation of Tom and Peter, it was difficult for the parents to acknowledge the twins' sense of mutilation of their identity, and their profound sense of loss of each other.

As the boys slowly recovered, they had a very changed experience of themselves, and their identities became fundamentally different from one another in a way that caused concern. At the end of the month, Peter, who had always been the more fretful twin, was the first twin to recover consciousness. He was no longer besieged by hunger because his new stomach now digested the food that he ate. Partially as a result of his new stomach he became less frequently distressed, although he was still mentally alert and very sociable.

Tom, who previously was the calmer, bigger twin, experienced the separation into two separate bodies, two separate beings, in a very different way from Peter. Tom had depended in a parasitic way on Peter, as Peter had lived for the two of them—frequently eating more to feed them both and crying out for caregivers to be present to be with them. Healthy looking Tom now began to shrivel like a leaf torn from a nourishing tree. He lost weight because he was lethargic and depressed and did not feel like eating. When agitated, Tom frequently turned to inanimate objects rather than calling out for his caregivers. In his separate room Tom seemed lonely and he isolated himself even further by not being very responsive or beckoning to his caregivers. We sensed that Tom was grieving the loss of his more socially and physically competent self, which he experienced as being located in Peter. It was as though Peter had held the mind for the twins, and internalized the thoughtful loving care of the caregivers. Peter had formed an attachment to the caregivers for the twins and now Tom had lost Peter. Even when, after a few months, the twins were placed back together in the same room, Tom seemed to fail to thrive. When the parents tried to feed Tom he regularly rejected their food. He was also rather worryingly slower in his physical developments and he seemed to retreat to not-thinking rather than struggling to overcome the habitual passivity he developed during the 11 months of his parasitic reliance on Peter's physical presence and Peter's sociable personality. It seems that "being two as one" often felt better to Tom than his new condition of "being two", of being a partially emotionally developed individual. It was painful to witness how the requirement to be a separate person was almost intolerable for Tom who had lost the best part of his self, Peter, who thought, ate and socialized on his behalf.

Rivalry and possessiveness of mother

Perhaps the problem for the conjoined twins, Tom and Peter, also gives an exaggerated portrayal of what siblings experience when simultaneously sharing mother's attention. It is universally accepted that babies experience a wish to be the only baby possessing mother, and the only baby possessing all that mother gives to the baby. Toys given by the mother or father often represent the mother or the father, or the parents. The excerpt below illustrates some of the conflicts and the resolution of conflicts surrounding sharing parents' love and care.

Peter and Tom: One year

> The boys, Tom and Peter, now physically separated, are in mother's bed, close to each other. Mother gives them each a set of multicoloured plastic keys. They both reach for the same set of keys. Each boy becomes determined to hold onto the shared set of keys. When the observer presents the spare set of keys the boys reject it. Instead they are even more insistent on holding onto the shared set of keys. Tom is so close to Peter that his arm rests on top of Peter's face and Peter cries in annoyance.

Does the key ring, given by mother, represent a part of mother and mother's possessions? Each boy seemed to feel that he should be the one and only baby with mother, receiving mother's gifts and possessing mother. There should be no difference, no obstruction to sameness and equality in mother's eyes. What was happening? Were Tom and Peter immersed in the conflict of searching for a new identity, or were they simply returning to the old emotional experience of being just one? What was evident is that they were discovering their emotional strength to overcome conflicts between them. In time Peter, who had eaten for the two, continued to struggle to face the emotional difficulties of interacting with his social network of nurses, parents, and siblings. On the other hand, Tom, when distressed retreated to the isolation of his own world. He adhesively clung to inanimate objects such as a dummy or toy that he could possess and control rather than bearing the anxieties of depending on another human for understanding and nurturance and facing the conflicts involved in sharing with his brother. Separation from his brother had been too traumatic for Tom.

The twin "as a primary caregiver"

Perhaps the fact that during the first year of life, Peter was continually annoyed, crying out in panic, evoking caretaker's assistance, had contributed to Peter's developing a better internal structure for facing emotional conflicts during the second year of his life. In the face of frustrations following his first year of life, Peter was obviously becoming both physically and psychologically stronger than Tom. Peter had also developed a remarkable love and empathy for Tom. In some ways Peter took on a "parent-like, supportive, thinking" role for Tom. Here is an example of this:

Tom and Peter: 18 months

> Tom and Peter were lying on their backs on a mat. Some building blocks were scattered between the children. Father was building a tower with Peter. Tom was spinning a top. He turned to look at Peter who had just put a block on the tower. Peter had just at that moment stopped his building and was just holding a red elongated building block and staring at it. Tom stretched over to take the brick in Peter's hand. Then Tom began desperately crying. It wasn't clear what he was thinking and Peter looked puzzled. After some time Peter used his right hand to give Tom the red brick. Simultaneously Peter used his left hand to pat Tom's shoulder tenderly in an attempt to soothe him.

Peter seemed very concerned about Tom's distress and in a loving gesture both shared his tower-building brick and comforted him. He had not abandoned his protective function towards Tom, despite their having been bodily separated.

Up to the time of the surgical separation, Tom had carried on living in a foetal state, living parasitically off the physical and emotional support of Peter. As a result when surgically and physically separated from Peter, Tom was not psychologically prepared to live alone. In fact, Tom's psychic structure resembled that of a newborn when exposed to anxieties. While still joined to his brother, Tom generally appeared complacent, and his anxieties and frustrations were not very noticeable—perhaps they were projected into Peter. Now that they had been separated, he did not seem to have the psychological resilience to mourn the loss of his brother and a part of himself. He had no emotional capacity to feel the conflicts involved in trusting his caregivers and experiencing them come and go. As a result, when momentarily distressed, Tom quickly protected himself by turning with increasing frequency to holding onto his dummy or other inanimate objects such as a toy. Unlike his care-givers, these inanimate objects could be possessed, controlled and "clung onto for dear life" (Bick, 1968).

It is difficult to know whether or not Tom, aged 18 months, continued existing psychologically in a conjoined state with his brother. At times, it certainly did seem that Tom's over-reliance on Peter, the more able twin, may have hindered the development of his own capacities for existing alone as an individual.

Tom seemed generally to be the twin who lacked autonomy and needed to be with Peter. Here is an example of this.

Twins: 16 months old

> The twins had their heads at opposite ends of the sofa. Tom was looking at a book with the observer sitting nearby. Peter was sitting next to his mother with a building block in his mouth. At one point Tom stopped looking at his book and stared at Peter for a few moments. Then he dragged his body towards Peter. After a few minutes Tom pulled Peter's leg against himself. Peter responded with a puzzled look. Mother asked; "What are you up to Tom?" Tom smiled at mother while remaining close to Peter's leg.

We were struck by Tom's trying to get physically close to Peter's leg, the leg that had previously been conjoined to his own body. If we think about Freud and body ego, one might postulate that Tom was trying to regain what he believed to be part of him, something that had been taken away. He is reluctant to take on the functions that previously belonged to a Peter who was intimately joined to him, eating, digesting, and linked with his twin's leg. If we think of the skin as an organ, which it is, we wonder what each twin might have experienced of the other twin's body.

Tom had the opportunity to either approach mother for comfort, or Peter, and he seemed to be very reliant on his closeness to Peter who was usually around. Peter frequently seemed agreeable to playing in the reciprocal role of the helpful or supportive brother. Who was the primary object for Tom? Was it his mother or was it Peter? Perhaps one of the consequences of mother and father coming and going for weeks at a time, was that Peter was the only reliable primary object available to Tom—not only did Tom feed via Peter's eating for him, but Peter was also available to comfort Tom or evoke caregivers for both boys at times of mutual distress. The twins displayed complementary teamwork as each boy performed different functions and used different complementary skills. Here are two examples of the twins' teamwork.

Peter and Tom: l6 months old

> Tom and Peter were both staring at a plastic ring resting on the floor. Peter stretched out and picked it up. He held it in his hand for a few moments before passing it to Tom, who had been looking on. Tom then looked at the ring in his own hand before beginning a long series of conversational sounding noises. Peter then smiled and looked at Tom and the plastic ring as though he had understood something about it from Tom.

Reciprocal play between the boys seemed to involve Peter as the director of a sequence of actions and Tom is the executor of the plan in Peter's mind. This is true particularly if the plan involved crawling or babbling which were abilities that evolved first in Tom, and subsequently in Peter, the stronger of the two after the separation. Here is another example of the boy's teamwork.

Tom and Peter: 21 months

> Tom and Peter were lying on their backs on a mat. Peter picked up a red ball and offered it to the observer with an implicit offer to play ball together with her. The observer caught the ball and rolled it

> back to Peter. Tom stopped building his block tower and smiled at the observer and Peter. Subsequently Peter threw the ball outside the play area. He then stared at the ball for a few moments, then looked at Tom. Tom meanwhile had begun dragging himself towards the door to fetch the ball for Peter and the observer.

Here it seemed that Peter and Tom were used to Tom tuning into Peter's non-verbal communications. There was something very touching about the boys' union. It felt as though it was an interdependent but loving togetherness, a togetherness that allowed a least some separateness.

The beauty and risks of "twinship" in infancy

With conjoined twins, the crucial human striving for a friend, a companion with whom one can deeply share some of the joys and sorrows of life, is met by the other conjoined twin. Burlingham (1952) and Bion (1967) both describe the phenomenon of the imaginary twin. Burlingham describes the conscious daydream of having a twin. She suggests that this fantasy occurs in the latency period as the result of disappointment by the parents who form a couple, leaving the child out. In the child's difficulty to face separation from the couple and loneliness at night, the child searches for a partner who will give him all the attention, love and companionship he desires from the parents, creating an imaginary twin companion. A conjoined twin may also be used similarly to an imaginary twin.

Despite the beauty of the early empathy existing between Peter and Tom, it is painfully apparent that there are risks present for both boys in the conjoint twinship and the "separated friendship". Firstly, it is obvious that in early infancy and childhood, the other twin can never be an adequate substitute for the mother and or adult caregivers. The infant twin cannot protect his twin, nor can he provide the emotional wisdom to receive and modulate the other twin's distress. Father and mother are necessary to maintain and to receive the boy's distress, bear the psychic pain and joy and think about these experiences in such a way that the capacity for mentalization is internalized by each boy (Fonagy, 2004). However, the other conjoined twin does provide some very crucial aspects of the human striving for companionship. The other conjoined twin is continually present, and experiences many of the same physiological changes linked with certain emotional experiences as does the other twin, since part of the body circulation system is shared. Also the other conjoined twin exists in synchronicity, since there are some shared parts of the inner and outer body, such as the Tom and Peter's legs, liver and digestive organs. A strong and empathic bond with the other conjoined twin allows shared complementary pleasures and inseparability in facing shared pains.

Bion (1967), in "The Imaginary Twin", describes how the dependence on an imaginary twin for projecting loving and capable or destructive and weak parts of the self, serves as an expression of the child's inability to tolerate a primary object that is not entirely under one's control. In this way the function of the real or imaginary twin is to deny the frustrations imposed by external reality. Projection of aspects of the self, whatever their nature, creates limitations on the development of the personality.

On bearing the pain of separation

Mourning the loss of the mother or father when they depart, bearing the oedipal jealousy of the parents being together, grieving over the loss of a part of the self through surgical separation from a conjoined twin, must occur. Twins are likely to make a closer bond to one another than to their parents and the separation of twins is experienced as an actual bereavement (Isaacs, 2007).

Inevitably for some time after being separated conjoined twins are subject to frequent minor operations to repair their bodies. For months after their surgical separation Tom and Peter's experienced frequent minor operations and minor illnesses. As time progressed it became apparent that it was not simply their physical health, but also primarily the relationship Tom and Peter had with their caregivers and their inner objects, that influenced the likelihood of progression in life, or regression into death. Peter, on a drip following minor surgery, points to the ball and window signalling to his father with his index finger that he wants to join his father in playing football outdoors. When father leaves, Peter cries inconsolably evoking his mother's wish to comfort him by patting his head in an effort to calm him. This is in marked contrast to Tom, who instead of crying to elicit his mother's comfort, generally retreats to the use of primitive protections against anxiety (Magagna, 2002). The following two vignettes depict the differences between Peter and Tom when they were recovering from painful minor surgery and had been separated from one another.

Peter, 21 months old

> The nurse was changing Peter's drip following some minor surgery. Peter was very distressed and flailing his arms about while crying loudly. Father was leaving the hospital with some of the older siblings who were visiting the twins. Father had a football that he was trying to conceal as he went out. Peter pointed at the football and then the window making impatient sounding noises. Mother and father smiled sympathetically at Peter for they had understood Peter's gestures indicating he wanted to go out with the father and the older siblings. Father said, "Come on, Peter, you are going to eat. I can't take you. Another day." Hearing this Peter put his hands over his eyes and cried inconsolably. Mother patted Peter and tried to calm him as father disappeared quickly.

Although in this subsequent observation Tom is younger than Peter in the above example, this vignette represents Tom's typical pattern of responding to separation.

Tom, 15 months old

> Several times, mother held a plastic transparent inflatable whale before her face and looked at Tom. Then she covered Tom's face. Each time mother put the whale before Tom's face he pushed the whale away and laughed. Mother kissed him then, and Tom made excited noises. Suddenly mother stopped playing with Tom and said she was going to make some toast for the older siblings who were having one of their rare visits to the twins in London. Mother smiled at Tom before leaving. He looked around the room and then towards the observer. The observer said his mother would be back soon. Tom whimpered as the observer told him that mother had gone to make some toast. He looked intently at the observer and smiled. Then he turned to the toy piano, which the observer handed to him. He made some noises by pressing some of the piano keys and then giggled. Somewhat later he retreated into himself by sucking on his dummy while staring for a long time at the fabric of his bouncy chair.

In this observation mother had suddenly left the room. In contrast to Peter, Tom did not cry or complain loudly about departures of mother or father. His lack of complaint about separations perhaps contributed to mother's not telling Tom that she was going away. It seemed that Tom was not able to hold onto his emotional needs and communicate them in such a way that the parents would respond. After the separation from Peter, Tom had not been able to find his own way of being assertive in struggling for emotional contact. He rarely initiated an interaction with an adult, although he did seek out Peter at times.

Food refusal: a rejection of life?

From the beginning of their lives, Tom and Peter were poor eaters. They were never breast-fed and when milk was offered to them by mouth they always refused it. When they were 11 months old they would scream for their turn to have a spoonful of solid food. Primarily Peter ate with Tom receiving the benefits of the digested food. After their surgical separation, they enjoyed the pleasure of holding onto a biscuit and throwing or messing with food, but at 11 months Tom still ate virtually nothing. Tom never had a physical abnormality making it difficult to eat. He simply shut his mouth tightly to the intrusion of a teat or spoon. Intrusions into his mouth seemed to be equated with the trauma of doctors, nurses, intrusive medical devices, and good caregivers turning into persecutory caregivers. Food became "a bad object" linked with the absence of the conjoined twin, the absence of the caregivers to protect Tom from pain, and the anxieties of separation. In *The Absent Object*, O'Shaughnessy (1964) describes children's reactions to separation from caregivers. She describes how the good mother is filled with protest, and rage about absence and turns into a bad persecutory object.

Since Tom was described as fighting for the spoon before the operation, one wonders if his world had turned more persecutory following the painful and traumatic surgical separation. This was a surgical separation that meant losing Peter who played such an important role for Tom's physical and emotional welfare. After the surgical separation, Peter detected the emotional and physically nurturing necessities, and ate and evoked responses from the nurses and parents, while Tom remained exclusively tube fed, a situation similar to having Peter eat for him before the separation. Tom did not seem to have the motivation or emotional capacity to identify his needs and awaken responses in his external caregivers. In discussion with the observer, mother realized that it was necessary for mother to "reclaim" Tom through actively engaging him and encouraging him to be emotionally present in his relationship with her.

Mother's attempt to reclaim Tom began before he left hospital. However, five months after leaving hospital, Tom choked on a piece of food and died.

Postscript

When he was six Peter returned to same hospital with his mother to have some further surgery. On this occasion Alessandra Marsoni, a psychotherapy trainee at the time, was asked to provide for Peter a weekly, hour-long "*special time*" in her role as a participant observer. On the first occasion, Peter is crawling using both hands and his one leg. Peter is immediately engaged with her and asks her to find the book, *Where is the Wally?* After the observer has found the book, Peter waits for her to turn each page. Peter tries to search for the missing *Wally* in the crowd. (The reader of the book is being asked to spot the missing child.)

Subsequently Peter spontaneously initiates another game in which the observer is requested to pick up a small apple on the floor. He then takes the apple from her and hides it under various cups that he has collected. He requests that the participant observer "find the apple". The observer is struck by how Peter was able to make use of her and elicit her attention in the very first meeting as well as in her subsequent meetings with him. He has such a capacity to express his emotions. This capacity for emotional expressiveness has been a crucial aspect of Peter's personality from the time he was born. It enabled him to engage with his caregivers and internalize their thoughtfulness in a way that helped him develop a more resilient psychological structure.

Peter's engaging personality also elicits mother's spontaneous free associations to his playing the game of "finding the missing apple". As she watches Peter's game, mother is spontaneously prompted to describe the separation by death of her conjoined then separated twin sons. She said, "Peter was desperate at being separated from his brother. He was looking for Tom all the time."

During the second meeting with the participant observer, Peter builds a staircase using only the green and yellow bricks. Peter subsequently uses his two fingers joined together to climb the staircase in a very pronounced way. Following this Peter violently hits the rebuilt staircase with a karate-like movement and the staircase breaks in two. The participant observer says, "Ouch" pretending to be the staircase. Then Peter firmly commands the participant observer to "fix it". On six subsequent occasions Peter requests that the observer make the staircase and then follow him with her two fingers as he uses his index finger and middle finger to climb up the staircase. As she is climbing the staircase, the observer is struck by Peter's use of his two fingers to go up the steps. She says to herself, "The fingers are "two in one", they share the same hand." On six further occasions Peter then breaks the staircase and insists that the observer "fix it".

After this repetitious play sequence is finished Peter embarks on another play sequence. He grabs a cushion and places it between himself and the observer. Then he hides behind the cushion. This is the beginning of a "hide and seek" game. The participant observer says, "I can't see Peter" and after a short-while Peter replies, "Because you must not see." The observer wonders if there is some denial of his brother's existence…or simply a continuing problem that he "can't see" his dead brother any longer.

When over the course of time Peter continues the previous game of breaking the staircase in two, the observer says, "Your play makes me think of you and Tom, when you became two separated babies instead of babies joined together." At this point Peter says, "What brother?" The observer says, "Your brother Tom." As if hit with the news of his dead brother yet again, Peter grabs one of the Sticklebricks and starts forcefully hitting his own head.

Following this Peter requests that the observer play "climb the mountain ". He instructs her to use her two fingers to follow his two fingers climbing up onto the newly constructed stickle-brick staircase/"mountain".

Various interpretations can be given to this repetitious play. What can't be disputed, though, is the fact that Peter repeatedly needs to elaborate upon his current anxieties regarding his dead brother, which create conflict within him. Klein (1932) would suggest that a particular theme in a child's play has to be repeated until the child is able to alleviate some of the inner conflict depicted in themes of the play. Peter's play sequence tells the story of two pieces broken, two pieces having to be put together, "two fingers in one hand" having to do something together. Peter's spontaneous play in the presence of the observer also repetitiously reveals his need to harm himself when thinking of his dead brother. The sheer repetitiveness of the play sequences suggests that Peter is trying to elaborate on some internal conflict to do with aggression to the brother and death of the brother. This death of the brother is accompanied by persecutory guilt requiring Peter to punish himself. Responding to this internal damage to the brother and then the self, Peter makes manic attempts to "climb to the top of mountain". "Climbing the mountain" must be done with the two fingers of the observer copying the two fingers of Peter joined together by the hand and walking side by side up the mountain. Since the family have the Catholic belief that people go to heaven when they die, there is an additional question: Is Peter excitedly avoiding punishment for the dead brother and "climbing the mountain to heaven and joining his dead brother whom Peter believes is 'up there' "?

In the ninth meeting Peter's play is more explicit. He asks the observer to hold an action man and "be Pedro". He also has an action man he calls "Gianni". Peter wants the observer's action man "Pedro" to follow Peter's "Gianni" action man as he drives very fast in his toy car. When Peter, with his "Gianni" action man beside him, arrives behind the bed, he gets out of his little red car, grabs the observer's doll, "Pedro", and hits him violently while making loud fighting noises. Then "Pedro" action man is left to lie flat on the floor. The participant observer touches the "Pedro" action man. Peter adamantly states, "He is dead.". The participant observer says, "You must be very sad now that you are all alone now.". Peter replies, "He is in the coffin." Then he starts repetitiously hitting the head of the "Gianni" action man, representing himself. As he is hitting he says, "Now he is dead too." He leaves the "Gianni" action man lying on the floor. Just as the observer is leaving, Peter becomes very subdued and hands the "dead Gianni" to her. In this action Peter seems to want to be looked after by the observer.

These meetings between the participant observer, Alessandra Marsoni, and Peter allow us to witness the death of Peter's two-year-old conjoined/separated twin. The death of his twin, Tom, which occurred while Peter was present in the buggy, still raises many questions for Peter: Did he kill his brother? Does he have to be punished as a result of some persecutory guilt and made to die too? Is this why he is unwell now and in hospital? Does he deserve to die? Can he stay alive although his brother is dead? Does he want to die to join his brother in heaven?

Later in his play Peter is able to reconstruct a stickle-brick version of his brother, but each time the issue of the dead brother surfaces in his play, Peter becomes very anxious. The process of working through his sense of guilt about the dead brother moves forward a little, but this therapeutic process with the observer is unexpectedly interrupted when the doctor abruptly sends Peter, in somewhat better health, back to the hospital in his country of origin.

What these vignettes illustrate so vividly is how essential it is to give a conjoined twin an opportunity to mourn the death of a dead sibling. Even though Peter had not physically hurt and killed his dead sibling Tom, it is clear that his destructive phantasies contributed to his guilt that he had done so. For this reason the local hospital was contacted to suggest further therapeutic work with Peter.

Conclusion

Gloria Dominguez's thesis describing her participant observation of the conjoined twins has raised important questions to be considered when studying the development of the personality. The conjoined twins, Tom and Peter, shared the same birth trauma of being separated from their physically fragile mother for 10 days while they endured many painful physical interventions to save their lives. Both twins were genetically extremely similar, coming from the same ovum. Since they shared part of the same circulatory and digestive system, they were at least partially subject to similar hormonal and other physiological changes accompanying their differing emotional states. Both had similar physical care from their hospital environment.

To what can one attribute the twins' distinctly different emotional responses to the same external situations after birth? There may have been different inter-uterine experiences for the twins, linked with their positions in the womb. Apart from this different positioning in the womb leading to different emotional experiences, can we assume that, although similar in many respects, each twin had inherent personality characteristics that were distinctly different? These differences in personality characteristics would then lead to differing responses from their caregivers.

From birth Peter seemed constitutionally able to express his distress, clamour for social interaction, show his frowns and anger when his needs were not met. He developed a more resilient psychological structure for facing conflicts in his second year of life when separate from Tom. From birth, Tom seemed more passive. The digestive apparatus shared by the twins was structured so that Peter ate for the two boys. Peter also complained and cried more frequently when distress was experienced and his cries served to beckon mother or father and the nurses to meet the needs of both twins.

By 10½ months, when the conjoined twins were surgically separated, Tom seemed to be parasitically living off the strengths exhibited by Peter. Perhaps Tom's strong attachment bond with Peter may have had a detrimental influence on his need to evoke caregiving responses from his parents and the nurses when he is distressed. In the absence of help from Peter during times of separation distress or emotional conflict, Tom retreated to inanimate objects such as his dummy or toys. Passivity in one twin who is living with a more capable and sociable twin can lead to hidden social deprivations for both twins. By the time they were 18 months old, Peter had internalized a more adequate psychological structure for bearing frustration than did Tom. Peter became the leader and protector for Tom who seemed to turn to him for comfort, for inspiration for play activities. Meanwhile Peter seemed to relinquish some of his own interest in a play activity in order to be a good supportive brother to his less emotionally adequate twin Tom.

Inherent personality characteristics and their effects on the caregivers, coupled with the reciprocity and division of roles involving splitting of healthy and weaker aspects of the personality, meant that Tom was more susceptible to having difficulties that he was not able to struggle to overcome. In the case of Tom, unfortunately, the consequence of his passivity and locating his emotional strength in Peter was death. In other instances, however, the consequence of passivity in the presence of a more potent, assertive twin can be serious emotional trauma, linked with the necessity of making fundamental personality changes when left to the task of surviving emotionally and physically as a person living as a unique and separate individual.

References

Bick, E. (1968). The experience of skin in early object relationships. *International Journal of Psychoanalysis, 49.*

Bion, W. R. (1967). The imaginary twin. In: *Second Thoughts.* London: Heinemann, pp. 306–10.

Burlingham, D. T. (1952). *Twins. A Study of Three Pairs of Identical Twins.* London: Imago.

Dominguez, G. (1994). Unpublished M. A. Thesis for Observational Studies M7 course. Tavistock Clinic, London.

Fonagy, P., Gergely, G., Jurist, E. Target, M. (2004). *Affect Regulation, Mentalization, and the Development of the Self.* New York: Other Press.

Isaacs, S. (2007). Personal communication.

Klein, M. (1932). *The Psychoanalysis of Children.* London: Hogarth Press.

Lewin, V. (2004). *The Twin in the Transference.* London: Whurr.

Magagna, J. (2002). Mrs. Bick's contribution to the understanding of severe feeding difficulties and pervasive refusal. In A. Briggs (Ed.), *Surviving Space: Papers on Infant Observation.* London: Karnac Books.

Magagna, J., Bakalar, N., Cooper, H., Levy, J., Norman, C., & Shank, C. (Eds.) (2005). *Intimate Transformations: Babies with their Families.* London: Karnac Books.

O'Shaughnessy, E. (1964). The absent object. *Journal of Child Psychotherapy. 1*(2): 134–143.

Winnicott, D. W. (1960). *The Maturational Process and the Facilitating Environment.* London: Hogarth Press.

CHAPTER FOUR

Twinship: a unique sibling relationship

Vivienne Lewin

Twins are siblings of a particular kind. While they share many of the aspects of other sibling relationships, there are other dynamics that make the twin relationship unique amongst sibling relationships. The particular qualities of the twin relationship are the result of two sets of factors:

1. The near identity of chronological age between the twins has consequences for each of the twins developmentally, in terms of both the ever-presence of the other twin in the minds of mother and father, and in the minds of the twins themselves.
2. The practical factors to do with the individual care of each infant. For twins there will always be a juggling of attention by the caregivers as the needs of each baby are taken into account at any one time. Inevitably attention given to one same-age infant at one moment will affect the amount and/ or quality of attention given to the other.

But there are also deeper unconscious issues that affect both the twin relationship and our perception of it. Twins both fascinate and disturb us, and we tend to attribute special qualities to their relationship. I believe that this special interest in twins arises as a result of developmental factors that echo our own earliest longings.

Our fascination with twins is linked with the universal urge towards twinning. The phantasy of having a twin is ubiquitous (Klein, 1963) and is based on developmental factors linked with essential loneliness, a longing to be known, and the creation of a sense of self within a primary object relationship. Both Winnicott (1953) and Bion (1967) describe the infant's illusion of creating the breast (its twin) in the (transitional) space created by the absence of, but essentially within, the infant's relationship with the mother. These very early experiences establish a blueprint for closeness and intimacy that underlies the longing for a twin self, as well as later more mature object relationships.

The specialness, with which we regard twins, stems in part from our narcissistic wish to be totally understood and at one with an object, as well as from a sense of the uncanniness of the double. Stories about doubles (Dostoevsky, 1846; Hogg, 1824; Saramago, 2004) centre around a sense of premonition of ill to come, of the horror and violence of the discovery of a double of oneself who has stolen our identity. The experience seems to presage emotional breakdown, as if a double represents the result of extreme splitting. Rank (1914) suggests that the double can represent the self, or aspects of the self—an alter ego. The double may be loved or hated, depending on what has been projected. It is essentially a narcissistic state of mind, and it may interfere with object love. While hatred and revulsion may be used as defences against the double, it can also be used as a reassurance against, as well as a representation of, death. As Rank suggests, it "finds its deepest foundation in the relationship with the mother" (p. 70).

While twinning may be regarded as a form of splitting, it is not necessarily destructive, as in the horrifying doubles described above. An alter ego may also be regarded as a close and supportive companion, such as the "daemons" in Philip Pullman's *His Dark Materials* (1995, 1997, 2000), or as imaginary companions that are so frequently used in childhood to provide support at times of developmental stress. The creation of an imaginary twin by the infant in its relationship with the breast, is essentially a creative act, and may well be the root of artistic creativity. I believe that an examination of both the general nature of twinning and of twinning processes as experienced by and exacerbated in actual twins, may lead to a greater understanding of developmental processes in both singletons and twins.

Twins excite all sorts of feelings and responses in others and are a source of considerable interest both scientifically and in everyday life. There are many books about twins. There are those written by a twin either to celebrate twinship, or to commemorate or compensate for the loss of a twin, either pre- or post-natally, at any and all ages. Parents of twins write about their experience of bringing up twins, both the pleasures and difficulties that they encounter. Scientists of all descriptions have studied twins for decades in the hope of learning the secrets of inheritability and the progress of both individual development and diseases. Children's books explore the many facets and functions of a phantasy twin through the twinships of the children in the story.

As a rather charming example of the universal urge towards twinning, I was told recently of a five-year-old boy with his father. The father was explaining to his son how a sundial works, and the importance of the shadow in telling the time. The boy said he had a shadow, and that his shadow was his twin. It went everywhere with him. He added that his shadow was not only was his twin, it was also his imaginary friend. But it was not his only imaginary friend, he explained—he had other imaginary friends like Teddy and some of his other toys.

In one sense I approach the subject of twins as an outsider—I am not a twin, nor am I immediately related to one. However, in my psychoanalytic experience as a transference twin, I am an insider with an outsider's perspective. As a psychoanalytic psychotherapist I have worked individually with a number of adult patients who have a twin, and through this route I have discovered the impact of the twin relationship on the psychoanalytic transference relationship. As a result, I have become particularly interested in twinning processes in both twins and singletons. The analysis of the transference twin seems to have been largely neglected in the psychoanalytic literature. I will outline in brief here the ideas I explore in depth in my book, particularly the creation of the twin in the transference and its implications for psychoanalytic work.

While the parents provide a developmental framework for each infant, relationships with siblings offer an opportunity to negotiate and manage peer social relationships. In fact, the existence of siblings propels us into having to confront issues that are not encountered in the parent–child relationship (Mitchell, 2004). The dynamics and tensions in the twin relationship are more intense than those in other sibling relationships, and are of a different nature from those between children and their parents. The absence of an age gap between the twins creates an inter-twin dynamic based on both a longing for sameness and an intense need for differentiation. The twinship lacks the developmental advantages offered by the age difference between non-twin siblings, but the twin relationship does provide an opportunity for unparalleled companionship and for an understanding without words, reminiscent of the earliest relationship with mother.

The existence of a twin may even ameliorate developmental difficulties in situations of maternal unavailability or neglect. However, a sound "friendship" is not necessarily a feature of the twin relationship. Many factors will affect how the twin relationship develops, and the extent to which each twin within the relationship develops a companionable rather than a narcissistic relationship with the other twin. Siblings and others may envy the closeness of twins, and the twins may use the twinship to create a barrier between the twin pair, isolating themselves from the parents and other family members.

I think it is important to state that I work from a basic premise that no two people are identical, not even monozygotic twins. To believe that they are identical is a defence against difference and separateness, whatever the genetic make-up of the twins. There are, to a greater or lesser extent, genetic, psychological, and behavioural differences between twins, as well as similarities. However, each twin has to struggle with his/her own processes of development to carve out a personal sense of identity. For each twin, this individuality will overlap to varying degrees with that of the other twin, and this may lead to aspects of a shared identity.

There are two central hypotheses that I propose. I will outline them briefly here:

1. *Twins are fundamentally affected in their emotional development by the fact of being a twin*

I am taking as a base the Kleinian view that the (unconscious) phantasies of the breast and of the parental couple are innate and are central to the development of each individual. Where then do the other twin and siblings fit in? I believe that the indelible twin relationship that is encountered in twins is linked with the infant's earliest experiences with both its mother and its twin, including during the prenatal period. The central internal structure that gives us a sense of identity would be developed through the infant's relationships primarily with its mother and, later, its father, and its acceptance of an oedipal parental couple of a different generation. For twins, this internal structure would be more complicated. (When I refer to the early dyadic relationship between infant and mother, I do not mean that father is absent, but that at this early stage father's function is to "vertebrate" mother, as described by Resnik (1995)). The maternal aspect has a containing function while paternal one has an organizing function.

The presence of the other twin leads to a situation in which mother and twins create a triad (prior to the oedipal triad), rather than the dyadic relationship that exists for singletons. As a result, for twins there would be three pair relationships: mother–twin 1, mother–twin 2, and twin 1–twin 2. The initial developmental process, say for twin 1, would be shaped both by the relationship with mother and by the relationship with twin 2. The relationship with twin 2 could theoretically be on a continuum between sibling rivalry and merging, and would include twin 1's perception of the relationship between twin 2 and mother. It is through this complex structure that each twin will develop a sense of identity.

If the twin bond is strong, it will interfere with each infant's relationship with mother. In addition, mother would be less available to each twin than she would be to a single baby. Whenever she relates to one twin, the other would be at least partially excluded. Placing father in the picture would create six pairs, and four triads, thus complicating the picture further. When mother and father are engaged as a pair, the twins would be excluded, and if awake, they would probably be an interacting pair. If the twins are together, even asleep, it is likely that they would still aware of each other. Awake or asleep, each twin is contributing to the formative experience of the other twin. Thus each twin has to engage with the processes of, and tensions between, separateness and relatedness to both the other twin and to mother, and later to father.

Separation from the other twin would be more problematic than separation from mother as the twinship offers a narcissistic refuge that lacks generational difference. At times when frustration may feel difficult to tolerate, twins would, to varying degrees, seek from each other some form of gratification, using the other twin either in phantasy or physically, thus filling the gap and avoiding the space that is necessary for the development of symbolic thought. Twins lack the maturity to be a true container for each other (Bion, 1962). The rather concrete nature of some aspects of twin relationships may be linked with this area of lack of symbolisation. There may be a confusion of ego-boundaries between twins and a relative and variable lack of a separate sense of identity. Most importantly, for twins, the twinning is not only an external phenomenon. The other twin would be a potent and active internal object, and would be a source of transference manifestations. The emergence of a transference twin in psychoanalytic work would lead to an intense and tenacious relationship between analyst and patient, echoing the internal twinship. This internal twinship is inescapable and lasts for the lifetime of each twin, even after the death of one twin.

The intense sense of closeness between twins is felt by twins to be a special and unique aspect of being a twin. The twin relationship may profoundly affect the resolution of both the early and later oedipal conflicts, thus having a lasting impact on the structure of the inner world of the individual twin. With the acceptance of mother and father as a couple that are not of the generational sameness as the twin couple, development towards the depressive position can proceed. Where such development is hampered, and where there is in any case an additional binding, internal relationship with the twin, problems are likely to ensue. The twinship may be used as a "psychic retreat" (Steiner, 1993).

The nature of the infant's affectional bond with the mother has been shown to affect the development of brain structures connected with emotional relationships (Schore, 1994). I propose that differential brain development ensues as a result of being a twin. With the inescapable presence of the other twin, persistent psychobiological patterns will be created between the twins and in each twin in relation to mother. These psychobiological patterns would affect all their relationships, especially the most intimate relationships in their lives, such as those between husband and wife, parent and children.

The internal twinship is a representation of the relationship with an actual twin, alive or dead, overlaid on each infant's twinning with mother in the earliest days. The internal twin object is inextricably linked with the "self", as are parental and other sibling imagoes. However, the chronological closeness of the twin pair leads to the development of a unique bond with a consequent internal object relationship that is of a different order from other object relationships. Separation from the internal twin may, therefore, be experienced as a threat to the integrity of the self at a primal level. Analysis of the twin transference would threaten the unity of the internal twin pair and may be resisted by the patient, even when desirous of separateness from the actual twin.

2. *Twinship is generally sidelined and treated as largely irrelevant in current psychoanalytic practice*

a) Despite Freud's (1900) recognition of the importance and permanence of sibling relationships in our internal world, twins and siblings have been rather neglected in psychoanalysis. As a result the presence of the twin in the transference is largely ignored, or is paid insufficient attention by many analysts. I propose that there may be two possible explanations for this lack of proper attention to the transference twin.

It may be that analysts underplay the significance of the twin relationship because they are nudged into a collusion with the (twin) patient who feels driven to maintain and to defend the twinship against any interference in it, even when overtly seeking to separate from the twin. Separation from the twin may be experienced as extremely threatening, even catastrophic, as it exposes the patient to a loss of known boundaries, with the consequent fear of dropping into a void or "nameless dread" (Bion, 1962a). This may result in a narcissistic collusion between analyst and patient, echoing the narcissistic twinship, and designed to maintain the "special" relationship between them and to cover up the painful and difficult developmental matters that are being avoided by the patient.

I will mention a few examples in brief:
Lacombe (1959) describes work with a twin patient whom he regards as having suffered from a mutilated identity as a result of being a twin. He describes how he doubled the length of session time to make up to the patient time lost, to restore to him his "full share" of attention, sacrificed because he was a twin. Instead of analysing the transference relationship with the patient, Lacombe enacted various roles assigned to him in the transference and explained why this was necessary to repair the damage done to the patient.

Ortmeyer (1970) postulates that twins suffer a personality deficit as a result of the experience of being a twin. He described a therapy with a twin patient where the therapist, himself a twin, enacts for the patient the role of the missing twin who speaks the patient's thought on her behalf, because she is unable to do so. He suggests that the patient suffers a deficit that can only be made good by such an enactment.

Burlingham (1963) describes the therapy of twin brothers Bert and Bill. This too involved the therapist in an enactment to get past an impasse he and his patients had reached. He justified this in terms of using the "Aichhorn Technique".

In each case, the therapist has explained in detail why he has deviated from standard psychoanalytic routine. However, I think that the tendency of some of the analysts to justify this sort of enactment supports the view that the analysis has reached an impasse, and there is a cover-up of a state that is too painful to recognise.

Thus, the enactment of the twin relationship in the transference may be the result of a narcissistic collusion against an experience of fragmentation. The inter-twin relationship has early and primitive origins affecting the sense of identity of each twin. The analysis of the nature of the twin transference in the consulting room may be experienced as, and may indeed be, a dismantling of a psychic relationship upon which the twin is relying for emotional security and identity.

Erotic relationships with siblings are not felt to be transgressive in the way that the oedipal situation is. Incest barriers between siblings are more fluid and less anxiety provoking than those between parent and child. Klein (1932) regards sexual relationships between siblings as a basis for adult heterosexuality. Twins and other siblings may turn to each other for physical or emotional comfort, or sexual exploration, in an attempt to avoid fears relating to the oedipal conflict. This may then add to the pressure for enactment in the consulting room of the twin transference, rather than its analysis.

It is important to distinguish between a transference relationship based on a twin relationship, and one based on the phantasy of a twin, as in the creation of the twin breast or imaginary companion. The twin transference in a twin tends to be intractable and is based on the indelible experience of a relationship with an actual twin overlaid on the early infant's longing for a twin breast. The phantasy twin of early infancy wanes with development, but persists in a modified form as a narcissistic core in all of us.

b) We believe that the parental relationship provides the framework for emotional development, and we tend to analyse in terms of infant/child–parent, as central to the analysis. It may also be that the analyst's recognition of the central importance of the twin relationship and hence of the transference twin, would lead to an experience of the analyst feeling threatened with a loss of parental authority and power. To "actualise" (Sandler, 1976) the transference twin involves the analyst in becoming, at least momentarily, a rivalrous clinging/conflictual sibling rather than a more distant and powerful parental figure with enhanced capacities for understanding. Together with the twin patient's anxieties about separateness and difference, recognition of the twinning and the creation of "sameness" between the analytic pair may cause the analyst considerable discomfort. It may, of course, also play into his/her own longing for a twin.

There is another perplexing issue that seems to occur almost without comment or question by either professionals or the wider public. I have heard of instances, most commonly amongst monozygotic twins, in which the twins are regarded, and regard themselves, as interchangeable as mothers. Thus we hear of a woman suing for the custody of her twin sister's child after the death of the twin (Segal, 2001) on the basis that the twin women are assumed to be genetically identical and, therefore, interchangeable. This notion ignores the fact of difference in genetically similar (not identical) twins who are developmentally each a product of both their genetic make-up and their unique experience of their environment and familial bonds. To suggest that we are no more than a product of our genes is genetic determinism gone mad.

I have also been surprised to hear a psychoanalytic discussion about a mother giving her newborn infant to her twin sister who had lost her own child, in which this "gift" raised no concern. Perhaps the rivalry in the twin mothers is appeased in this way, but the "gift" is made in the face of the fact that the infant is the child of one, not both mothers. Perhaps it is a function of our fascination with the nature of the twin relationship that such actions seem to raise little comment. The delusional belief embedded in the idea that twins are interchangeable, notably as mothers, is based on a lack of differentiation in both the twin pair and in the public eye. The twin mothers are seen as having achieved the perfect, universally longed for state of "at-oneness" with another. It is as if twinship has been elevated to a magical sphere where reality is ignored and the "rules" regarding relationships are unique.

I think the terms "identical" or "non-identical" twin are useful only in relation to the underlying psychic dynamic processes that are active at any particular moment, rather than to describe the genetic status of the twins. While there are certain to be differences in the development of each of these types of twins as a result of their zygocity, I have found that the emotional processes explored in analytic work do not particularly reflect this difference. Twinning processes go on in each type of twinship and are reflected in the transference relationships with the analyst and in many other relationships.

The analysis of the transference twin and the origins of this transference relationship deserve particular attention. It is important to understand more fully the processes involved in the twin relationship from a psychoanalytic point of view. Where an analysis of the twin transference does not take place, an essential aspect of the twin patient's developmental experience and relationships will be left untouched and "un-understood". I believe we do need to take note of the developmental processes in relation to twinning and twins; the underlying dynamics in analytic work with twins and the associated transference phenomena; and the enduring nature of the twinship.

References

Bion, W. R. (1962). *Learning from Experience*. New York: Jason Aronson.

Bion, W. R. (1962a). The psychoanalytic study of thinking. *International Journal of Psychoanalysis, 43*: 306–31.

Bion, W. R. (1967). The imaginary twin. In: *Second Thoughts. Selected Papers on Psychoanalysis* (pp. 3–22). New York: Jason Aronson.

Burlingham, D. T. (1963). A study of identical twins—their analytic material compared with existing observation data of their early childhood. *Psychoanalytic Study of the Child, 18*: 367–423.

Dostoevsky, F (1846). *The Double*. [Reprinted 2004 London: Hesperus Classics].

Freud, S. (1900a). The Interpretation of Dreams. S.E. 4.

Hogg J. (1824). *The Private Memoirs and Confessions of a Justified Sinner.* Oxford: Oxford World Classics Paperback [1999].

Klein, M. (1932). *The Psychoanalysis of Children*. [Reprinted London: Hogarth Press 1980].

Klein, M. (1963). On the sense of loneliness. In: *Envy and Gratitude and Other Works*. (pp. 300–313). [Reprinted London: Hogarth Press 1980].

Lacombe, P. (1959). The problem of the identical twin as reflected in a masochistic compulsion to cheat. *International Journal of Psychoanalysis 40*: 6–12.

Lewin, V. (2004). *The Twin in the Transference*. London and New York: Whurr.

Mitchell, J. (2004). *Siblings. Sex and Violence*. Cambridge: Polity Press.

Ortmeyer, D. H. (1970). The we-self of identical twins. *Contemporary Psychoanalysis, 6*: 125–142.

Pullman P. (1995, 1997, 2000). *His Dark Materials*. Warwickshire: Scholastic.

Rank, O. (1914). *The Double. A Psychoanalytic Study.* [Reprinted: 1971. North Carolina: the University of North Carolina Press].

Resnik, S. (1990). *Mental Space*. London: Karnac Books.

Sandler, J. (1976). Countertransference and role-responsiveness. *International Review of Psychoanalysis 3*: 43–47.

Saramago, J. (2004). *The Double.* London: Vintage.

Schore, A. N. (1994). *Affect Regulation and the Origin of the Self: The Neurobiology of Emotional Development*. Hillsdale NJ: Erlbau.

Segal, N. L. (2001). When twins lose twins: implications for theory and practice. 10th International Congress on Twin Studies, London July 2001.

Steiner, J. (1993). *Psychic Retreats. Pathological Organizations in Psychotic, Neurotic and Borderline Patients*. London: Routledge.

Winnicott, D. W. (1953). Transitional objects and transitional phenomena—a study of the first not-me possession. *International Journal of Psychoanalysis 34*: 89–97.

CONFERENCE 2

CHAPTER FIVE

Siblings in development: towards a metapsychology

DC = David Cohen (Chairman)
JM = Juliet Mitchell
RB = Ronald Britton

DC opened the conference outlining that, at the first conference in April, we spent the day considering twinship and the ways in which being a twin and the innate tendency to twin, can affect the way we relate to ourselves and to others. This conference centred upon what might be considered to be at the very heart of the matter; the place of sibling relations in psychoanalytic theory and practice. Juliet Mitchell and Ron Britton would discuss these matters both between themselves and with the audience. Starting with **JM** each speaker was invited to open with a short statement outlining their thinking on the subject of siblings and the roles they play in our inner world.

JM explained her particular angle and interest in siblings, rather than talking about a particular area of sibling work. In particular, she did not get to her ideas about siblings through siblings per se, either through an interesting case of sibling transference, or a sibling relationship pre-eminent in a patient's inner world. Instead she was working on hysteria and thinking there was something missing in the accounts of hysteria, and finding to her relief that Anna Freud thought the same. Hysteria is the founding illness of our discipline and it still remains the founding "illness", providing the basis of our area of work, the unconscious; it also gives us the main aetiology of our discipline; that mental illness and health are on a continuum so that we use the pathologies of ill health to show us the other end of the spectrum. Given this primary place of hysteria in psychoanalysis, **JM** was concerned that it is the male hysteric always goes missing and considering this absence of the male hysteric took her into reading in anthropology, history, as well as psychoanalysis. This led her to siblings.

Suddenly the Oedipus complex shifted and she became aware of children dancing around. She went back and re-read her own clinical work and all the major case histories of hysteria, and found siblings popped up everywhere. It is that "everywhere-ness" that is both the importance and the interest in siblings, and also the weakness from a psychoanalytic point of view. Looking back in the history of sibling presentation in psychoanalytic work, it is apparent that they are everywhere and nobody has noticed. Closer scrutiny reveals that everybody has noticed, but what happens to them? They come and go. This parallels male hysteria as well—it comes and goes, it is everywhere and nowhere.

JM drew our attention a crucial paper after the First World War, to illustrate this absence. She refers to this paper in her second book, *Siblings, Sex and Violence*, in a different way from her thinking today. The paper is called "A man's unconscious phantasy of pregnancy in the guise of traumatic hysteria—a clinical contribution to anal erotism" (Eisler, 1921). He discusses a case of male hysteria. It is fascinating because the patient is the eldest of 14 children, and his eldest sister was born when he was six and his youngest sister when he was already married and an adult. His response to the birth of the two sisters triggers his disturbance as a child, so to speak, the beginning and the end points of his hysteria. He was a tram driver but he had had accidents, so he was moved to being a conductor. He had an accident himself that tended to show that, in fact, he had not had what he, as it where, acted having—traumatic hysteria. He actually had hysterical fantasies of giving birth—the subject of the paper.

Eisler notes that all these brothers and sisters, in all 14, had a lot to do with his disturbance. That was 1921. Later, in 1956, Jacques Lacan rewrote the paper for Eisler, in his way of telling people what they should have done. In re-writing it, Lacan tells Eisler that he shouldn't have gone off into ego psychology and he was quite wrong to stress the anality of the birth. However, Lacan doesn't mention the siblings at all. So we have 14 siblings with Eisler and none with Lacan, and that is an illustration of our work on psychoanalysis with siblings. They are either everywhere, in which case you can't really think about them, or they are nowhere.

There is a lot to be said about the "everywhere-ness" of siblings, but you can only chart the everywhere-ness of siblings. You can't actually think analytically if something is everywhere or nowhere. For Lacan, they cannot be thought about, and you don't even know that they are in the case history. If you had just the Lacan reading of this case history, we wouldn't know that this hysterical tram driver was the eldest of 14. Approaching it not through siblings but through hysteria, can we bring siblings in from either nowhere or from everywhere, into a metapsychology? We have to bring them into an analytical way of thinking about them to see whether they really do contribute to unconscious processes. We know that the oedipal complex and castration fears, and repression, bring up unconscious processes. We know from Klein and Winnicott and Bion and others that there are unconscious processes in relation to the mother. Do the relationships between siblings matter, or is it only, say, between siblings vis-à-vis the mother?. Do the relationships between siblings, and, therefore, relationships within the sibling transference, actually produce pre-conscious or unconscious processes? Are we getting symptoms that take their origin from the sibling nexus? Are we getting unconscious effects from the sibling nexus, or are we only getting pre-conscious effects, which are not, therefore, distorted and which allow free access through a little bit of hard work, but not through our methods of free association which is always key psychoanalytically? We have a phenomenology of siblings, but not a metapsychology. Looking at a horizontal axis—siblings, cousins—the main question is: is that horizontal axis also productive of unconscious processes in and of itself?

RB thanked **JM** for making him think. He had been thinking about siblings while he was working with a patient. A patient brought a dream in which she, really exemplifying a lot of work that had been done in analysis, was in the fast lane in a car and had overtaken another vehicle in the middle lane, which seems to have had an accident of some sort. Having passed it, she, in a very complicated way, had to reverse that car to come back to this wreck and to try and rescue it. This exemplified the problems of this patient, in her life, of this going backwards. He had taken that up and in response to his interpreting that she was having to go back and not overtake the damaged person, she suddenly reported something that her father had told her that as a child. The patient was the youngest, and she had an older sister. The patient was very precocious and a precocious talker. Father reported that "something funny happened to you and you went backward, and we think it was something to do with the fact that your sister who was older than you couldn't talk". This example of not looking at sibling relationships generally is an indication of not working out some metapsychology regarding siblings.

RB felt that his being an only child would partially explain it, but added that even he has cousins. He knows from one of his patients that in the Balkan languages, the word for brother or sister and cousin is the same. We have grown to think of the Oedipus situation as being an intra-psychic and not simply an experience of life. Where are siblings in that configuration?

What about Freud's later idea of primal fantasies? Did he include anything about siblings in those? Actually he did, of course, one notable example being his idea in *Totem and Taboo* of the primal horde, of the brotherhood, the brothers who murder the father to take his place. It also drew attention to the fact that this idea of Freud's doesn't surface as primal fantasies until quite late, but even in his correspondence with Fliess, he was talking about something called endopsychic myths. So this links with the question, do siblings have a place? In Bion's terms for instance, are there pre-conceptions of siblings? There are pre-conceptions in Bion's theory of breasts, of the

Oedipus situation and of a number of things. He doesn't of course have a closed list, but it would raise a question, and that would imply, that even if he didn't happen to have siblings, psychically speaking you would have the preconception of a sibling and you would be looking for something to fill that. Do we find that anywhere? We do in Klein actually. Klein talks about unborn babies. For somebody like Melanie Klein, **RB**, as an only child, would be regarded as a child murderer who had prevented and abolished the unborn siblings. So, yes, siblings are around everywhere, and it does introduce something contentious. We find the same tension in psychoanalysis as well as in other areas.

The brotherhood is a familiar phrase and the sisterhood is familiar particularly since the feminist movement. **RB** recalled that as a child his father belonged to the brotherhood, which was a church. Actually he only belonged to it in order to play in the orchestra because he was a good musician, and to sing in the choir. It was the Plymouth Brethren in this particular instance, and in the nonconformist churches in the North of England, the term "brother" and "sister" was very frequent. It is these lateral groupings of people who are hostile to vertical hierarchy of Bishops. So even in the religious meetings there has always been this tension. We find that the same tension in psychoanalysis as well as in other areas. Is there an expectation of conflict between those who are going to adopt some sort of hierarchically organized metapsychology and those who might adopt a more lateral one?

He free-associated to these thoughts about these relationships to the writings about the tribe of the Danakil. The Danakil were the most famous and ferocious tribe in a particularly remote part of Ethiopia. As an initiation right of the men as teenagers, they had to kill someone, and they were not initiated until they had killed. They killed strangers. Interestingly, they also castrated them and they kept the castrated genitalia as trophies, and they regarded as virgin men those who had never killed. They were obliged to marry their first cousin. Incest with the brother or the sister would have been very much taboo but there was an order. The man was expected to marry his father's sister's daughter, and if you couldn't manage that, in default, it would be your father's brother's daughter—i.e. the first cousin. This linked with what seems an extremely hypertrophied sense of the "other" as hostile stranger. They have to marry nobody more remote than their first cousin, and they kill strangers. Is it something that we are we trying to contain all the time in the sibling area—creating boundaries around sex and aggression?

The trade unions are always talking about brothers and sisters. In the religions, the Shakers form a single house as brothers and sisters, and address each other as brothers and sisters. But outside marriage they had no sex. They didn't think they needed sex because they were convinced the second coming was going to happen in their own generation. Both sexes managed to be in the combined brotherhood and sisterhood, unlike the nuns who are an example of sisterhood or the monks as the brotherhood, but the Shakers had to exclude sexuality—they made furniture instead.

In our prioritising sibling relationships, is there opposition to parenthood, and do people tend to divide as to which their allegiance is going to be, even metapsychologically?

JM tried to bring together these random thoughts. As regards Bion's notion of the pre-conception, if we have a pre-conception of a sibling then we are within her field of metapsychology, because that means there is something there that is a universal, that is likely to have unconscious effects—a pre-conception or primal phantasy of a sibling. In one sense the primal phantasy of the primal scene is a fantasy of the sibling, and it becomes a fantasy of one's self because the siblings starts as one's self. One thinks that the baby that's coming is going to be more of one's self, and the shock is that it is somebody else. That is the big sibling trauma, the big dethronement, the reason we get a sort of hysterical reaction in children with the terrible twos, because they have been dethroned.

Thinking of Eisler's case as a focal point, there is something which both Eisler and Lacan take as illustrative of the castration complex; in an incident when he was three plus years old, the tram conductor refers to his "youngest brother" (it's "youngest", not "younger", suggesting there was probably another brother, between the tram conductor, the patient, and his youngest sibling). In this illustration, the three-year-old patient is at the dishevelled end of the breakfast table, and his mother is nurturing his youngest brother. He stretches across the table to pick up a piece of bread that his father has left on the table, to grab it for himself. His mother throws a knife at him, which luckily enough goes through his hat. He wears a little cap that Hungarian peasant children in the earlier part of the twentieth century wore, and the knife goes above his ear and through his hat. The mother is horrified at what she has done, rushes him off, puts him in the position that you put baby in across the bottom of the bed, so as to see that he is not wounded, and sews up the hat, typically with red thread. It is all rather beautiful, and here we have the beginning of his castration complex, which leads to his hysteria.

What, might we imagine, is the mother doing? She is in a state of primal maternal pre-occupation. She is feeding another baby. What Winnicott calls separation anxiety is most effective if there is another baby there, or, if you think there isn't another baby there because it is your fault that your jealousy has done so much you have got rid of it. Melanie Klein's case of Erna shows that it's rather worse if there isn't a sibling to reassure you that you didn't kill it. She suggests that we should have more siblings, not less, because if there's nobody to come along, there is no one to reassure us that we haven't got rid of them. Winnicott suggested that only children have no siblings to come along to reassure them that they haven't been murdered.

In this scenario, we see a mother suckling her new baby in a state of primary maternal pre-occupation, and her toddler aged three, does something to distract her. She reacts from inside that maternal madness (in Winnicott's terms) and throws a knife. It may be extreme, but we have lots of extreme cases that we deal with. Maternal violence is common as Estelle Weldon demonstrates well enough at the Portman Clinic. Because his mother is pre-occupied with the baby, the presence of the sibling is the real nodal point, about separation anxiety. So it is not only that that is a castration image—of course it is, and it will go on to become one, even if it isn't at that moment. At that moment, there is also a sibling relationship, part of sibling nexus. This sibling, who has taken his mother away completely—she really is embedded in that primary maternal pre-occupation—that sibling is somebody the toddler hates.

JM puts the sibling trauma before the oedipal castration phantasy —the sibling complex occurs between the mother–baby of Klein or Winnicott or Bion, and the oedipal castration of Freud, Lacan etc. She places it between those two as an independent complex. In bringing the sibling nexus out from everywhere or nowhere, she starts with sexual curiosity. This occurs when a child thinks its mother ought to be pregnant because that is what it perceives of a neighbour, and a friend's mother, or because something in her is beginning to dissociate and move away from the child who begins to suspect another baby. All sexual curiosity starts around that. The first thing you think of when you wonder what is in your mother's tummy is actually yourself, but yourself as another, so you are thinking always of yourself as a narcissistic extension to that baby. When it actually comes, when you get a knife thrown at you, because the baby has got the food and you haven't, you begin to know it is not you, and that provokes the violence. Violence, war, and rape also occur on a horizontal axis.

RB suggested we use the mechanism of splitting, to express something forbidden in relation to our actual sisters, and instead we kill somebody else's sisters. So the sisters of the enemy, as it were, become the prey.

As regards the story of the toddler, the mother and the stealing of the bread, the food, the weaning of the toddler, and the mother, is such a battlefield. At that moment when she is in this maternal mode, none more so than during primary maternal pre-occupation, it's interrupted and then we wonder whom the toddler is, at that moment, for the mother? At that moment does she cease to be the mother of the baby, in her own mind? Is there a history to that, too? Is there a brother in **her** childhood? Who is she throwing this knife at? If the mother was the patient, one would be thinking along some sort of lines like "who is this little monster that has suddenly appeared", which would have been a child if she had managed to stay in maternal mode. Is she pushed back in her own sibling relationship? Women, in particular, experience direct shifts between being daughters, mothers, sisters, and wives. With the mother and the violence of that interruption, anything that interrupts this primary pre-occupation is always felt to be violent for the two parties concerned.

JM referred to a small study in Western New England, about 10 or 15years ago, in which first time mothers were asked who they saw their newborn baby as, in terms of their past history. Some said they saw a replication of themselves, but the majority said a sibling. So it is quite likely that the baby that you see is your own past history, a sibling. Winnicott suggested that the mother hates before the baby hates. Perhaps this comes from that little sibling, and the violence felt towards that sibling that replaced you, re-seen in the newborn. It is very common to call your child by your sibling's name, quite revealing perhaps.

RB noted that while **JM** had convincingly described the hostility that can be generated by siblingship, everything she has written about it implies attachment as well as hostility. Perhaps that too is something rather primary. At the same time as we are describing the murderous intention towards siblings, actually what we witness quite a lot is people devoting their lives to saving siblings or the successors to siblings as if to rescue them or to save them. Freud's comments about rescue fantasies suggest that for a man to have a rescue fantasy, the woman he rescues is his mother and for the woman to rescue the man, he becomes her child. It is inferred from what we are saying we should take reparation very seriously in Klein's sense of the word—there is going to be quite a lot of reparation going on to the sibling figures which may influence a great deal of what goes on in the way of care in the world.

JM suggested this may be reaction formation. Looking at the infant's reversal into the opposites of love and hate, we note an incredibly quick switchback effect between hate and love that occurs because the origin lies in narcissism. You think this baby is more of you, and everybody calls you the baby and is talking about you, as far as you're concerned. But then there is this baby which isn't you. Your love for it is narcissistic but not necessarily in a negative sense, because it can then extend into love for itself. But at origin it is a narcissistic love that does not develop in the same way as love of parents does. There is something different about this, shown in how quickly the love/hate moves. Pre-conscious splitting is very useful though it may later become pathological. What we do is hate the enemy and love our brother and sister. The original splitting relates to the same person. You love and hate the same person—sibling ambivalence is all and it can easily come back. This dynamic switch between love and hate in siblings also occurs in e.g. Bosnia with the reversal into opposites in a very forceful manner—your best friend next door becomes your worst enemy.

RB noted the narcissistic quality of sibling love. Considering the Danakil, the most narcissistic thing you can do is to have to marry your first cousins, in the sense that you are emphasising the blood, the common shared blood. This is apparently a necessity in this situation because you kill anybody you don't identify with. This is a very extreme version of what I think is rather basic. There is a basic hostility to that which is absolutely "other", with which there is no identification. While there is oscillation with the siblings, the sibling is not otherness, it is not another tribe, but it can be the absolute prototype of the non-self. The history would then be elaborated around this, and as suggested, the inclusion of thinking about the arrival of younger siblings, which is so potent for so many people. Just at a point where, anyway, the difference between the self and others is developing, and the struggle of ambivalence is part of that.

JM suggested that we need to explore narcissism in a slightly different way and we might get more material from group analysis than we get from individual analysis. The degree to which an unconscious rapport develops with another member of the group is striking. Bion talks about pairing within a group, and perhaps that is the way we need to look at the extension of narcissism, into understanding others horizontally. This is what Winnicott called the "ecstasy of friendship". We often get revolutionary situations where the horizontal comes into its own as in the women's movement in the 1960s and 70s. Those moments are ecstatic and create a sisterhood like that pairing in a group, but it is more extensive than pairing. It is a real extension of narcissism into the other and it is not a negative—it is a social bonding. It can then explode into its exact opposite—the hatred comes in as well. You are in a sense enlarged by having brothers and sisters, in the cognitive sense.

RB linked this experience to the fact that it was the FA Cup Final today as an example of what it is like to have an overwhelming feeling, at the same time as hostility, the two going together; that to be part of that you just feel as though you have merged with a mass of some sort, and united in a sort kinship, an ongoing relationship, and a mutuality called supportive. We are suggesting that the ground on which the sibling relationship might stand, if it is primal like certain other relationships, can be utilised. There may be all sorts of kinship unions—sometimes it is local, but they may not be at all local; sometimes you get everyone born in one village, or it's everybody who is clan related, or it can be everybody who has the same idea. What seems to be particularly human is our capacity to form clans, or kinship unions, at an intellectual level and not simply at a blood level.

JM suggested that having a sibling is a very necessary catastrophe. You have got to have one, or you have got to have a substitute for it in some sense.

RB qualified this, suggesting that it depends where you are at the moment. Taking his own position as an only child, having a sibling might be redemption. The catastrophe would be the non-appearance of the sibling.

JM agreed that we may think the catastrophe is what we have done.

RB added this was right, so you don't see the second coming.

JM: "Does make you wonder about Christ, doesn't it?"

RB said that these catastrophes are very individual as well.

JM agreed. We all have a sibling trauma. There is a universal situation. At some point we are utterly displaced, and that is the final stage of what is seen as annihilation, nameless dread, all the ideas of the primary annihilation that the helpless baby has with its mother, the terrible fear of being annihilated, if it is dropped, if it is left etc. That is pre-psychic, a state of bodily distress and despair, and terror. It becomes psychic with the sibling, the original primal dread is re-enacted, when you actually think somebody who you thought was you, isn't you.

RB described two cases he was very impressed by, looking back in the light of what **JM** had said. The dominant figure was the already dead sibling before the birth. The leitmotif of such a patient, eventually when we get down to it, is "I should never have been born." "I was not intended to be born"—and both patients spoke all the time in their analysis, of their brother who died before they were conceived, that lived really so strongly in parental mind. There is also the misfortune for some people of being born into existing history, as it were.

In response to a question from the floor regarding the role of envy in a relationship with siblings, **JM** spoke about the three terms: rivalry, jealousy, and envy. Envy has had a lot of attention with Klein and in relation to the mother. Rivalry is what we normativized in sibling relationships. Jealousy is the concept we have left out. We have not done enough work psychoanalytically on jealousy. There are very good papers by Freud and others, but it has been displaced, perhaps by the excellent understanding of envy of the mother. Jealousy is more to do with who you are than what you have, or that "you are in my place", rather than "you have my things". Iago hasn't got the place he wants, he is overwhelmed by jealousy. He is envious too of what goes with that place, but actually the primary green-eyed monster is jealousy, because Othello was where he wanted to be. That is what you get in marital partnerships, rivalries, and jealousies. Perhaps we have some anxiety about looking at jealousy. Jealousy is a lateral thing as well, and in Freud's paper on paranoia and jealousy, he did indeed have an older brother who is the trigger of his jealousy.

Perhaps envy of siblings is pre-conscious. The jealousy seems to actually have much more disturbing unconscious roots. The roots might have to do with this sense of annihilation, that you don't exist if somebody else is in your place. If your partner is with another person you are annihilated in a sense.

Thinking about siblings via hysteria, it is the disappearance of the self, the disappearance of subject, the sense that you are not there, that you actually don't exist; and originally it's the helplessness of a baby, "if I am dropped, I won't exist". This has not been sufficiently incorporated in our understanding of hysteria, although both Jones and Lacan in different ways talked about it.

Secondly, it becomes "if that person is me, I don't exist", and in jealousy, if you imagine yourself in a situation where your lover is with another person, it is you that is popped out of the picture, and it may lead back into the jealousy of the primal scene. Are you there in that moment of your own conception, or is it just your parents that are there? You can do it vertically that way, but it is also there horizontally. Thinking of the tram conductor again, if that baby is where I think I am, and I am not, it is somebody else at my mother's breast, then I don't exist. You see it in all the sorts of literature of children at that age when a baby comes along. It is when the false voice comes and the false self can start much earlier, in a sense, against the misconceptions of the true self. But you actually see and hear children becoming quite false in themselves after the birth of a sibling. They start using high pitched voices and being super good, or they are pinching and doing horrible things behind your back so you don't see it, but it is there and it is that you are so jealous, because you are not there.

RB suggested that **JM** was talking about an existential anxiety. To go back to Lacan, it seems that what she was saying was like the question "for whom you do not exist". It takes us back to Lacan's mirror phase and his idea of the identity of the child actually being made by the mother in his image, standing behind the child. It does capture the infant's being in the eye of the mother, and it is this that ensures the sense of identity of that moment. So with the arrival of the other sibling, it is not simply that you lose care and rivalry for the breast, but you also lose being the centre of the mother's gaze.

JM again raised the question, "Is there a dynamic in the nexus of siblings that can give us something that we can think about in terms of unconscious processes?" Taking the mirror phase, what we are saying is that Lacan's baby looks in the mirror, first of all a mirror in virtual, so your ego is never really a truly reflection of yourself—it is an inverted reflection. Then it is the mother who stands there and says "that is Johnny", so for Lacan it is always alienated, though not for Winnicott.

There is another mirror in this too, the mirroring that children and babies in particular do. If you watch a very small baby and people coming into the room, the excitement is for the sibling, the older child. Absolute passion. Not for the mother or father or whoever else it might be, the passion is for the other child. You will push a child in a pram down the street and a small toddler goes past or a school child goes past and they are in ecstasy for that child. So that is a real mirror reaction, not an alienated mirror reflection. What comes across is actually something about what we have that is the same. There is something in the containment of that child's movements, which are nevertheless excited. What Lacan talks about is the mirror being, or giving, the Gestalt to the unco-ordinated movements of the baby. A child has a co-ordination that is not the same as the placidness of the adult. It is a containment of excitement in the child's movement that seems to be what we are looking at when we are looking at the sibling mirror reflection. So you are not looking at the same mirror reflections. We need another dimension to our picture of narcissism, another dimension to our picture of the ego, which goes towards that lateral horizontal group, which is more about the sameness in children, that they love and that they are passionate about.

RB spoke of unrequited love and explained that he was thinking of two little boys, where there was such passion in the young arrival for this older brother—but it was not reciprocated.

JM recalled two adopted children that she once watched. The little boy, aged about two, saw his older sister, about seven or eight, across the beach and he RAN passionately towards her and she gave him the most withering look and he fled. He shrivelled up—he sort of vanished, in that disregard.

RB wanted to give "envy" a better run. He said he was thinking of the origins of envy as Milton thought about it, which is when Lucifer becomes Satan, when God announces that his only son is Christ. The line is "The Christ is announced", and at which moment Lucifer feels himself impaired. At that moment as his idealised self, Lucifer thought he was the ego ideal; he thought he was God's ego ideal yet the ego ideal is the parental ideal. And this announcement meant that he wasn't and just had a part to play in it. This is where envy comes in. There is great jealousy, but it is envy in as much as it is a terrible hostility to the being of the other person and the identity of the other person, not simply to their position or what they possess and their attributes that have just been announced, which makes so much trouble.

On the matter of place in the family, **JM** suggested that analytically, the youngest child is like the only child and always wonders where the other one is. The issue of birth order is not terribly open to universalising. It is not unimportant, but one might think about whether it is always the next one that is the real problem, the one that you next expect that is the real problem, whether it becomes less important as you go down the line. Freud thought everyone was a repetition and he knew he had lots of sisters. Everyone was a repetition of the first awful Anna that he had, not the dead brother, but the live sister. The dead brother was a problem too. An older child can very much want the third one. **JM** described a friend whose little boy of four, Jacob, has a two-year-old brother, Timothy, and they are expecting a third. They knew it was a boy, and the older one, Jacob was talking to the two-year-old, and talking to his mother all about her pregnancy and the new baby. She is a doctor and she is very intrigued and a little bit surprised at quite how curious he was, and so she said to him "well would you like to come with me to my next ultrasound and you can look at it and see it and I can show you?" He said, "Oh no, I just want Timothy to know how awful it was when he was born."

JM suggested that although the oedipal and castration complexes are universal, this doesn't mean to say that the forms they take always the same. It means that there is something in that prohibition on a relation, on an incestuous relationship, which is universal. It may be a brother/sister prohibition, where the sister is the carrier of reproduction, as among the Trobriand Islanders that Jones and Malinowski have argued about. Whoever is the carrier of reproduction will be banned from the child, whether it is the sister or the mother and in that sense there is a prohibition on incest that is universal. That prohibition and the need for repression gives you the fact that all those desires become unconscious and come back to you as symptoms in a described distorted way, come to you in dreams and so forth. The question is "is there something universal between siblings?" **JM** thinks that there is. And that is that we all don't only grow up as babies of mothers, we all grow up having to be replaced. That is the condition of humanity, that we are not omnipotent, unique, omni-competent, only ourselves. And the aim of any analytical therapy of any sort is to understand that awful experience that "I am not unique. Because, oh thank God—other people are like me, or I am like them." The ordinariness that you get at the end of clinical work is to do with what the siblings' nexus can give. That is as universal as the mother/infant relationship. You have got to be unique and omnipotent in that baby–mother relationship when you are completely helpless. Later on you haven't. It is primary but it is universalized.

On the issue of cultures in which older siblings, either male or female, take care of the younger ones after the age of two, **JM** noted that this was relevant for us, the fact that it is not always the mother who is there, even from the very, very early stages. It is a big political question as well as a psychological one. It is a universal that we have mothers. We do have fathers too. That's a universal as well, even with sperm banks, and surrogate mothers. There are still eggs and sperm that they come from. The question really is addressed to "are we putting our emphasis right between birth and caring?" And, of course, most of the psychoanalytical literature would always say, even somebody like Bowlby, "I mean the carer", and Winnicott certainly did. But that carer may be not the mother from birth onwards, and that goes for adoption and fostering too.

So far what we know about sibling caring is that it tends to be rather autonomous in terms that it may be consciously modelled on what a mother might do, but it tends to be something that is decided by the parent about how siblings should look after children. Nevertheless it works itself out in ways that is actually to do with the sibling dynamic. It isn't just an imitation of mother or an imitation of father. The boy is the big brother, and the girl is the big sister, not that she isn't also the little mother, but there is very much a sibling dynamic again at stake in that relationship, which is variable. Regarding siblings in clinical practice, it is common to think "oh yes, your sibling is the next person in the waiting room", but not to consider oneself as big sister or little sister. That is missing still though we pay a lot more attention to it now. We don't have the same theoretical model, so we hear once again the older or the younger sibling, and not something that is intrinsically a dynamic itself. We have to do it from within our own work in a sense. But it isn't there; there isn't a model for it yet. It is terribly important. We should not terrify the people by insisting that really they must be worrying about their mother and father when they are not, they are worrying about their sister and brother. We need to talk about listening to one's patient.

The issue of foster children was raised. What was the impact on the children living in foster families, i.e. the relationship between birth children and foster children?

JM described a programme by Phil Frampton who wrote a book called "Golly in the Cupboard". He was brought up in Barnado homes and was fostered out from time-to-time with the possibility of adoption, which never worked. His argument was that he did not want to go all out for fostering or even adoption, but particularly not for fostering, because the fostered child gets moved and loses the peer group community, and the continuity of that peer group in the school. Even though he was in a Barnado's home where there was child abuse, literally physical and sexual abuse, nevertheless, as a middle-aged man he still has his friendships from the home. This issue was overlooked by suggesting that institutions were bad and families are good. What we have not seen is that the institution replicates another aspect of life in a family, which is the horizontal aspect, and how powerful and strong and important that is. The fostering he regards as very, very negative and he suggests that even in a bad home, his lateral relations were extremely important.

RB questioned whether we are talking about biological factors, or universal factors, and what do we mean by this, as opposed to the vicissitudes and particularities of the situation. The maternal object is not necessarily the objective mother, and who should know that better than an analyst. It doesn't matter which sex you are, you can be the maternal object in the transference, or the paternal object in the transference, or you might be the sibling, or you might be the partner. It is a movable feast. Maternal pre-occupation is an issue for which **RB** has a great deal of respect. Being a man he needed to get it via analysis and having had a lot of maternal patients, rather than just his own experience. As a father, perhaps one is rather rivalrously sceptical about the unique position of the mother.

He has come to think, for instance, that maternal pre-occupation is a biological state. It is quite an incredible state, actually, if you have patients you have seen through it, and it has its own time, its own schedule and that fantastic degree of attention to which the child is so extremely sensitive about the fluctuations. Women will often testify that they didn't know this was going to happen, they didn't realise what it was going to be like and they couldn't have imagined it was going to happen. So it would be a shame if people missed out on that.

JM raised the issue of wet-nursing vis-à-vis maternal preoccupation. The baby was handed over immediately and she suggested that maybe the wet nurse also has maternal pre-occupation.

RB agreed that the wet nurse would be in that state of mind.

JM thought that maternal pre-occupation is not necessarily linked to the actual biological mother, but it may be biologically linked to motherhood.

RB added, "and to maternal function".

JM: "through lactation and all the other hormonal things".

RB spoke about the extraordinary practice in Jane Austen's family, a pattern that was just accepted. The children were breast-fed, kept until they were just about to become toddlers, and then they were sent to the village to be brought up in the family of the village women who had children of the same age. They returned to the family at about five or six. So that would have been Jane Austen's experience—an extraordinary experience it must have been thinking about siblings, because this was all in a village where the children that they lived with during this toddler period were the people they met in the street. Those links were actually preferred, and across the class boundary too. Our society isn't so characterising the way we like to represent it. And in Africa we meet families where the older sisters brought up the children.

JM addressed the issue of gender and the distinction between gender and sexual difference, in response to a question about a type of adulthood that is gendered but isn't sexually differentiated around procreation from two sexes, male and female, masculine and feminine. Sexual difference is what we do get from our old model of the Oedipus complex, castration complex, and what it is to be a girl who wants to father the baby from the father, and what it is to be boy who wants to grow up and be like daddy and have a replacement mother. This is there for reproduction, and its prohibition. But along the sibling line, along the horizontal axis, there is, of course, reproduction. The tram conductor is a perfect example. He reproduces babies at the drop of a hat in his hysterical fantasies, and so do the children when their mother is expecting another baby, when they are expecting a sibling. That is exactly the age when children are always giving birth, they are playing doctors, and they are playing mummies and daddies. Perhaps we have been misled by calling it "mummies and daddies". It seems that what they are actually producing is "a baby from myself". This is a parthenogenic birth, a hysterical birth. Parthenogenic birth goes back to **JM**'s interest in siblings from the point of hysteria, because of the hysterical births. It maybe be a perfectly two-up, two-down marriage but the psychology of it as a hysterical birth, is parthenogenic and the hysterical dimensions of birth will be reflected in patients. It is parthenogenic, it is narcissistic, and Eisler talks about it as a narcissistic birth.

For unconscious processes, the process of society, of civilisation itself, there are rules, there are prohibitions that set up unconscious processes and there are prohibitions which aren't only the prohibition of the castration complex on incest with the mother, or the reproductive agent, if it is the sister, in the Oedipus complex. There are prohibitions from what **JM** calls, ironically and jokingly, the "law of the mother position". You cannot kill your brother or sister. There is a law and what is being said to the sibling is, yes, you feel murderous towards this brother/sister, but actually you can't kill it, and that is a law that has to be taken on board. There is also a "law" that comes in at that point which is not identical to the one of the castration and Oedipus, which says "OK, I know you want to give birth and you are playing mummies and daddies and doctors but actually it is me, the mummy, who gives birth", and it relates to the difference between generations. The oedipal castration also sets aside generational difference. Before that we get a generational difference between a child and the adult—only adults can procreate. The child has to learn, and it does learn, and it does become unconscious, unless it becomes a hysteric with those phantasies that return. It cannot give birth from itself, parthenogenically. We are getting from our lateral relations from our horizontal axis.

Where siblings become the carers, the issue of how to bring up your sibling is taught in the community. It is actually not just instinctive or random, it is actually proscribed and there is quite a lot of castigation if you don't do it well and you don't do it properly. It is regarded as pretty important. To go back again to this point about primary maternal pre-occupation, there has to be for any baby, some sort of primary maternal pre-occupation, whoever it comes from. No baby would survive without it. There is work on premature babies and what that means, in terms of absence, if the baby is in an incubator, of primary maternal pre-occupation. Apparently there is a high degree of psychosis. A child from the age of five onwards can be a sibling caretaker, usually not much before four or five, but it is fairly unlikely that a four or five-year-old will be anything much more than a imitative little mother. What is necessary is a real primary maternal pre-occupation from somebody. The baby wouldn't survive without it.

In terms of the question as to where the sibling nexus is situated between the mother and Oedipus, it is the group that this sibling nexus goes into. The baby doesn't wake up to a world in which it sees only breast. The baby comes into a world in which there are a lot of other people too. It hasn't formulated its world-view as a group but it begins to formulate it in the sibling nexus.

JM referred to her use of "seriality" for the siblings in the group. We learn that we are one in a series. It raises the question of what the younger baby means to the older one. The younger one comes into a world where there is something who is like itself, a sibling, a child of the same, or at least the same mother if not both parents, who has been there before it was born. And again, a "non-it"—there's an absence of "it" quite early in its conceptualisation. Here is somebody who is my parent's child, just like I am, so where was I? We need to put in this other dimension between its time coming in, and between the flatness of the vertical horizontal model, to get a perspective that looks inward.

RB returned to *Paradise Lost,* and Milton's exploration of this problem, of the "fall". God announced the existence of the Son of God. The distinction in theology is between this one figure and all other figures, including angels, of which Lucifer was chief Archangel. That this figure was not created, "begotten, not made" is a mysterious phrase, but it means that he never did not exist, and Lucifer rebelled (or Satan rebelled) against God at this point and his first argument is "there was no time when we, the angels, did not exist. Who says we are creations?" Of course, the rebuttal is, yes, but you are creatures, you were created. Then along comes the next lot of creatures, Adam and Eve, as the children of God in another sense. So this issue about whether you always existed, privileged only in Christ, or whether you were created seems to be enough to turn the world upside down.

JM: suggested it was not only the angels, it is every child until they have a sibling. That is exactly what you think. You think you have grown like a plant has grown; you were there last year and you were there the year before, and before that. I think you do believe you are always there, that is part of the necessary omnipotence.

RB spoke as someone who managed not to have a sibling and hopefully somehow came to terms with his mortality and the fact that he didn't always exist. He suggested it must also be a developmental crisis, therefore, into which the sibling may play a part. The maturation and development of knowledge, which is of course the downfall of Adam and Eve later, is also a factor in these situations. I think for some it's as if it comes too soon and that the arrival of the sibling might be a premature arrival of what was going to develop slowly. Maybe by the time you are 10, you could get your mind round it. But what if you're only 13 months old or something like this, perhaps what would be developmental then becomes traumatic?

JM described a discussion at a conference in Milan between Jennifer Johns and Winnicott, JJ said she was going to have another second baby and she asked Winnicott "what would be the best age for my eldest child for me to have the next one?" And Winnicott just said "no age".

So we have different problems, different difficulties. The point is not the sibling; the point is your annihilation. And that happens along the ley line so to speak. It happens developmentally, it happens around that age at which people talk about separation anxiety. That's when it happens, but it's repeated throughout our lives. It is what is happening in war, it is why we kill and rape, because we might be killed and raped.

Linking with the idea that the infants between 12 months and 36 months will be aware if there is a miscarriage or an abortion, **JM** recalled that Joyce McDougall relates slightly differently to that. She was watching a session of Winnicott at Paddington Green, in which a mother from the East End, with no psychological sophistication, has a terribly disturbed child who had gone crazy—just pre-toddler. Mother brought him, and he was indeed crazy, rushing all over, breaking everything up. Winnicott said to the mother, "have you told him about the baby you are expecting?" The mother looked completely aghast and horrified and says "nobody knows", and nobody did know because she didn't dare tell her husband because her husband would have wanted her to have an abortion because it's too soon after the last one. Winnicott said, "Well, your son knows, try and find the time within the next two weeks in which you can talk to him about it, and I will see you again." It was one of those instant cures.

A member of the audience raised the issue of honour killings. It is sanctioned by the culture and by at least one of the parents, it's carried out by the male on the female, and wondered how does this fit, where a sibling is allowed to kill another one legitimately and have perhaps the father colluding with it and sanctioning it.

RB explained he had no first hand experience of that, but it does bring to the fore immediately the primacy of the group. There's the family as group. To break the family law, group law, is punishable by death, whatever the circumstances. It occurs in non-familial groups too, with gangs for instance. The group process as a manifestation, of a pre-conception, is so powerful. One of Bion's points which was always in the background of his thinking was that, whoever you are, you are relating to a group all the time. You are positioned in some sense or other psychically in relation to an invisible group. It was bringing to the fore the enormous power of that, and that the group takes onto itself a power none of the individuals in the group ever would. It is characteristic of the group behaviour in general, and something we have to beware of. To give an example, he [**RB**] was always very suspicious of admission committees because they develop a degree of knowledge and certainty that none of the individuals would possess as individuals, but it as if one can acquire greater wisdom by becoming a member of a group which shares ideas. One never would lay claim to it as an individual either. The legitimacy of group aggression seems to come from the assumed power of the group, and in certain circumstances things become legitimate which no one individual perhaps would perpetrate.

DC thanked the two discussants, and the audience for their active participation in a lively discussion.

References

Bion, W. R. (1961). *Experiences in Groups*. London: Brunner Routledge.
Bion, W. R. (1970). *Attention and Interpretation*. London: Tavistock. [Reprinted London: Karnac Books, 1984].
Eisler, M. J. (1921). A man's unconscious phantasy of pregnancy in the guise of traumatic hysteria—a clinical contribution to anal erotism. *International Journal of Psychoanalysis, 2*: 255–286. (This text is commented on by Jacques Lacan in his seminar on the Psychoses, during the meeting of March 14, 1956: see below.)
Freud, S. (1901b). *The Psychopathology of Everyday Life*. S.E. 6.
Freud, S. (1913). *Totem and Taboo*. S.E. 13.
Klein, M (1932). *The Psychoanalysis of Children*. [Reprinted 1980, London: Hogarth].
Lacan, J. (1956). *The Seminar Of Jacques Lacan: Book III. The Psychoses*. Ed. J.-A. Miller (1955–1956). [Translated by Russell Grigg. New York: Norton 1993].
McDougall, J. (2003). Commentary on anaesthesia or psychotherapy: eradicating thoughts or working them through. *International Journal of Psychoanalysis, 84*: 211-215.
Malinowski, B. (1915). Ethnography of Malinowski: Trobriand Islands, 1915–18. London: Routledge.
Milton, J. (1667). *Paradise Lost*. [Reprinted1964, New York: Washington Square Press.]
Winnicott, D. W. (1958). The capacity to be alone. In: *Maturational processes and the Facilitating Environment*. London: Hogarth Press. 1979.

CHAPTER SIX

Sibling incest

Prophecy Coles

> "Children of the same family, the same blood, with the same first associations and habits, have some means of enjoyment in their power, which no subsequent connections can supply; and it must be by a long and unnatural estrangement, by a divorce which no subsequent connection can justify, if such precious remains of the earliest attachment are outlived." (Jane Austen, *Mansfield Park*, 1814)

It may seem strange to begin my talk with this quotation from Jane Austen, but I want to use it as my base point, or "lighthouse"[1] as I step into the troubled waters of sibling incest. Austen's insight into the precious nature of the "earliest attachments" between siblings highlights the distress or disturbance of mind that must take place if there is an "unnatural estrangement". For as Austen writes in *Mansfield Park,* and in many of her other novels, "the conjugal tie is beneath [the] fraternal" (p. 244).[2] So I shall be taking the paradigm of sibling incest as an extreme estrangement between siblings and my inquiry will be addressing the question as to what has gone wrong for sibling incest to occur.

We have tended, in our psychoanalytic theories, to ignore the association between adult sexual behaviour and what Freud (1907a) called the "immature erotism" (p. 46) between siblings. There has also been a failure to think further about Klein's (1932) early insight into what she calls "the secret complicity" between siblings that, "plays an essential part in every relationship of love, even, between grown up people" (p. 244). In this talk I shall be returning to early Freud and Klein and suggesting that if "the connections" between "children of the same family" are running smoothly, and the immature erotic attachments are not distorted by sadistic wishes, siblings give back to each other a particular reflection that no other relationship "can supply". I shall then be suggesting that if, for any reason, there is an "unnatural estrangement", we can expect to find this loss manifest itself in destructive behaviour either towards the self, or towards others, and in some cases, or at least in the case I shall be presenting, sibling incest may occur. It needs to be noted that I am generalizing from one case, and this one case only reflects the problem of incest from the male side.

I shall begin with the case history of sibling incest. Mr D was a South American student who referred himself to an outpatient clinic where I worked, and I saw him once a week for a year. The time constraint upon the therapy necessarily means that I do not have a finely detailed understanding of the structure of his inner world. However, I look back on this case as providing a beginning for Mr D, though with hindsight there is a lot that I wish I had explored.

Mr D's presenting problem was that he was depressed following the break-up of a relationship with his girlfriend. I am going to illustrate the therapy in terms of three stages, though, of course it was neither as clear or as easy as the way I shall describe. The early sessions concentrated on the loss of his girlfriend and on his depression. His girlfriend had left him, he said, because she thought, "I wanted someone to worship me." As we explored what his girlfriend might mean, he began to reveal a feeling that he "puffed himself up like a bomber jacket" because he felt empty inside.

The second stage of the therapy went back to his childhood, and was almost exclusively concentrated on his relationship with his father. Mr D's father had lost his own father in early childhood and

Mr D was expected to replace his grandfather in his father's mind and help to heal the unmourned loss. In his early years he seemed to live up to his father's ideal that he should become a distinguished academic, like his grandfather, for Mr D was a clever young man. However, as adolescence approached he experienced his father as engulfing him and stretching out tentacles that might harm him. The path that had been laid out began to rock perilously, as he inwardly screamed, "I do not want to be an academic like my grandfather." He left home precipitously and came to England to study engineering.

The exploration of his difficulties with his father led into the third stage of the therapy, in which he revealed that he had sexually abused a younger sister. The "sexual abuse" that took place between Mr D and his sister I am now going to call "sibling incest". In the NSPCC (2000) guidelines on sibling relationships, sibling incest is defined not only by the occurrence of sexual penetration but also if, "fondling, mutual masturbation, digital penetration and oral-genital penetration" occurs and where there is at least a five year gap between the siblings. Mr D was five years older than his sister, Miss D, and when he got to early adolescence he "fondled" her and masturbated in front of her a few times.

As we began to re-construct the reasons that Mr D might have had for the "incest" in early adolescence, the mother's part in the family dynamics became more significant. Mr D's mother never became alive in the therapy as had his girlfriend and father. In fact, a terrifying deadness could sweep across the therapy when she became present and Mr D would be unable to say anything and I would have difficulty in concentrating. I suspected this feeling was linked to a mother who was finding her children difficult to manage, for at such times I would certainly have difficulty in understanding him and thinking about the sibling incest.

An early image that Mr D had of his sister was of her sitting on a rug and crying. I had a physical feeling of desolation as he described this scene, and I felt he was communicating a shared sibling experience of neglect. He said, "She was horrible. I treated her like the younger boys at school." I am not sure what he meant by that except to suspect that he had wishes to bully and hurt her. However, from the slightly hectoring tone that he could use as he talked about her, I believe he was expressing his hatred of his own sad baby self. The sibling relationship shifted as they became older and he remembered games they would play in which the two of them would hide. Sometimes the game would be to hide in their father's study and hope that they would not be found. A significant memory, that seemed to link the games of hiding with the later sexual acting out, was when they both ran away from their mother when going on a walk. They got lost and they were not found for several hours. They became, in Mr D's words, "suffocatingly frightened". Mr D reported that it was this image that came to his mind when he remembered masturbating in front of Miss D. It was believed, by all the family, that Miss D was her father's favourite child. She had, however, a difficult relationship with her mother. There were many fights and arguments and her mother is reported to have said to Miss D "I wish you had never been born." Miss D's animosity to her mother united the two siblings, for Mr D also felt that there was little place for him in his mother's affection. "My sister did not want to be like our mother. She refused to accept the family's way of communicating." And then Mr D was able to add, "I am beginning to see that I also refused the family's way of communicating. My sister and I have a lot more in common than I realised. We both felt rejected."

I do not have a clear picture of the "family's way of communicating" except through the emotional experience of being with Mr D. Mr D was at his most lively and most distressed when he spoke about his ex-girlfriend. He was most angry when talking about his father, and he was at his most cut off and un-communicative when we approached his feelings about his mother. From this picture I imagined a parental couple who had, in a lively and hopeful way, conceived their children. But they had foundered on the task of bringing them up and keeping the children's needs in mind. Their own difficulties or narcissistic needs intruded too much and consequently the children lost their way (Faimberg, 2005).

Mr D inwardly collapsed at the approach of adolescence. He needed to challenge his father in order to discover his own way forward into potent male adulthood, but he did not believe the father would survive if he refused to carry the burden of unmourned grief. He was not able to confront the task, and instead he resorted to incest as a concealed form of attack. There was, however, a more grief-ridden aspect to the incest. I believe he enacted a double loss that he had already experienced. He was angry and distressed at the loss of a father who could not respond to him as a son, but he was also frightened that the narcissistic mirroring that his sister had given him was slipping away from him as he faced adolescence. As we have already seen, Mr D and his sister had formed a couple as they hid and ran away in early childhood. But it was a couple that made them "suffocatingly frightened" for they were also in need of parental attention. The failure of parental attention had meant that their sibling relationship had had to do too much work. He needed to be worshipped, for he felt empty inside, she needed an ally against her hated mother. These narcissistic needs overburdened the sibling relationship and it broke down as Mr D struggled into adolescence. Their more hopeful childhood games of being lost and found turned into a destructive attack upon "the family system of communicating" and the tragic result was that the sibling relationship, which had been the most nurturing for them both, broke down following the incestuous incidents.

At the end of our year's work Mr D was back again with his girlfriend and this did not feel a regressive move, for I believe that the girlfriend represented an aspect of the sister that had brought some comfort and necessary mirroring to Mr D in his early childhood. However, Mr D also indicated that he would still have a rocky path to climb. He brought the following dream in our penultimate session. He was with his family. Miss D had red marks on her face, which turned into tentacles that stretched out and Mr D felt in danger of being enfolded by them. He ran away to his grandmother's house where he met his girlfriend and they found food in the grandmother's kitchen. I believe that the Medusa-like image of Miss D, with a damaged face that spread its tentacles towards Mr D, had many layers of meaning in his inner world. The link with the father is clear though he is also able to discover a nurturing grandmother in his internal world. Miss D is still troubling him. She is damaged by him and then becomes a dangerous object to him psychically. We shared the knowledge that the self-absorbed father, the depressed mother and the damaged sister were still sources of extreme anxiety for Mr D, and we both knew that, like Perseus, he still had a long journey to make if his internal Medusa was not to turn him to stone.

I am going to leave the clinical material there and turn to the question of the paucity of clinical material on sibling incest. There is little clinical disagreement that sibling incest, just as parent/child incest, is an indication of the breakdown of a family system. The few case histories that one can find in the literature generally suggest that both victim and perpetrator are left with feelings of guilt and anger (Forward & Buck, 1978; Volkan & Ast, 1997). However, in a recent publication "On Incest: Psychoanalytic Perspectives" (2005) there was nothing on sibling incest. One of the contributors, Monique Cournant-Janin wrote: "I shall concentrate on parent–child incest, leaving to one side any discussion of brother–sister incest—even though the latter easily lends itself not only to displacing and inflecting the prohibition but also to toning it down, *since it does not transgress the difference between generation*" (Ibid. p.65. italics added). The point of quoting from one of the most recent publications on incest is to confirm that sibling incest does not find a bibliographic entry in most books, whether they are on child abuse or child development or incest. Even in a book that alerted us to the importance of sibling relationships, The Sibling Bond by Bank & Kahn in 1980, there is no entry on sibling incest though there is some clinical material. The majority of reports on child sexual abuse suggest that parent/child abuse is the most common (Herman 1992. Waterhouse & Stevenson, 1993) though this is contradicted by the most recent NSPCC report (2000) in which sibling abuse predominates. But we have to turn to Freud and Klein in order to understand more generally why sibling relationships and sibling incest play a small part in the theoretical and clinical concerns of psychoanalysis.

In the early works of Freud and Klein there is a belief in the importance of sibling relationships in the psyche. For instance Freud (1907a) wrote a paper on Jensens's Gradiva about "the development of a love ([and]...the inhibition of love) as an after-effect of an intimate association in childhood of a brother-and-sister kind". And he goes on to add, "It is in attachments such as this, in combinations like this of affection and aggressiveness, that *the immature erotism of childhood* finds its expression; its consequences only emerge later, but then they are *irresistible*" (p. 46 italics added).

This idea that the psychic consequences of early sibling attachments irresistibly emerge in maturity brings Freud close to Jane Austen's view that I quoted at the beginning, though I do not think that Freud would have agreed with Austen's conclusion that "...the conjugal tie is beneath [the] fraternal" (Mansfield Park. p. 244). He was, however, still tussling with how to find a place for sibling attachments and their influence upon later adult sexuality when, four years later, he wrote a paper on the psychology of love. "It sounds disagreeable but also paradoxical, yet it must nevertheless be said that anyone who is to be really free and happy in love must have surmounted his respect for women and have come to terms with the idea of incest with his mother *and sister*" (1912d. p.186 italics added). It is not clear in this passage whether Freud conceives of the incestuous desires between siblings as having an independent place and a separate structural effect in the internal world to that of incestuous desire for the mother. However, if a distinction is to be found between incestuous fantasies for the mother and the sister, which I am suggesting there must be, how might we conceive of this difference theoretically? Freud seems to overcome this theoretical difficulty a few years later in probably the most famous case history of sibling incest, The Wolfman (1918b). The Wolfman's obsessional neurosis, Freud insists, was caused not by his incestuous relationship with his sister but by watching the primal scene when he was resting in his parents' bedroom at 18 months old. And from then on, it seems, siblings and their incestuous desires play no part in Freud's structural theory of the Oedipus complex, except as "second editions" (Colonna & Newman, 1983) of oedipal desire.

Something very similar happens in Klein's thinking. Early Klein (1932) endorsed the view that the "early immature erotism" (Freud, 1907a) of sibling attachments "are irresistible" when she wrote that sibling relationships contain powerful infantile erotic "phantasies" that "play…an essential part in every relationship of love, even, between grown up people" (p. 224). Her argument for this view is more complex than that of Freud, for she believes that sibling love, and even sibling incest, can give a necessary experience to siblings who are finding their conflict with and hatred of their parents too difficult to manage. However, Klein abandons this view about the healing quality of early erotic passions between siblings as she strengthens her argument, in her later writing, for the importance of the pre-oedipal mother. In both the examples, from Freud and Klein, something important gets lost as they shift away from their earlier beliefs about the strength and importance of sibling relationships. In the case of Freud, we have no structural model of the manifestation of the "irresistible" brother–sister love in adult life, except as a "second edition" of the oedipal one. When Klein seems to abandon what she calls "the secret complicity" between siblings that can have "a favourable influence upon the child's object relations and capacity to love" (pp. 118–119). we lose the idea that there might be two complementary and creative developmental lines that intertwine and offer separate internal models of love and hate; the vertical line of our relationship with our parents and the horizontal line with our siblings.

I want to keep in mind Freud's belief in the "immature erotism" between siblings and Klein's belief that the erotism of sibling relationships can be healing and can "play an essential part in every relationship of love, even, between grown up people". For without an understanding of the powerful infantile erotic fantasies that accompany sibling relationships, we will continue to hide sibling incest under the cloak of Oedipus, and as a phenomenon it will continue to be left unacknowledged in our clinical writings.

One way of finding a place for sibling relationships in the structure of the internal world is to go back to the myth of Narcissus, but not the version that Freud favoured. Freud took Ovid's myth in which Narcissus rejects the nymph Echo. The gods decide to punish him by giving him, in turn, the experience of unrequited love. He sees his own reflection in a pool of water and falls in love with it and he dies, pining for the mirror image he can never obtain. Freud and subsequent theorists have used this myth to describe narcissistic pathology. However, one result has been that we have tended to look at narcissism with what Kohut (1986) called "a negatively toned evaluation" (p. 61) and have neglected "the adaptive value of narcissism" (ibid). The myth that psychoanalysts have ignored is Pausanias' version. "Narcissus has a twin sister. On her untimely death, Narcissus suffers unbearable pain. This pain disappears fleetingly one day when, contemplating himself in a lake, Narcissus believes he sees his sister's image" (quoted by Tesone (2005) p. 63). In the Ovid myth there is no mention that Narcissus might be searching for an aspect of the self that is associated with an "other", who is symbolised by the idea of a twin.

Vivienne Lewin (2004) has most forcefully brought to our attention in her book on *Twins* the idea that if one is a twin, that relationship dominates the internal world. But the fantasy of being a twin also holds a universal appeal that is usually understood as representing a wish to return to the womb. As therapists we are familiar with the times when there is a regressive wish, in our patients, to return to a place of womb-like safety. But there can also be times when this regressive wish has a different feeling tone. It is not so much a need to be held safely in the wordless shelter of the mother/therapist, as the wish to share a secret moment. This moment can be experienced as seductive and subversive as it stretches into a challenging area of mutuality. The dominant fantasy in this psychic space is that the lost double may be found with someone of the same size who will share the same feeling, as in Pausanias' version of the myth of Narcissus. I believe that it is this experience Klein (1932) is referring to when she writes of "the secret complicity" between siblings.

For a more detailed understanding of this wish to be reflected in "the other" who is felt to be the same, I am going to turn briefly to the work of Stern (1985). In his book The Interpersonal World of the Infant he suggests that from birth there is "an organizing subjective experience" (p. 7). The salient point that I want to emphasize is that it is no longer possible to see the newborn infant in a state of "primary narcissism" as Freud (1915c) described. The infant at birth can differentiate between its mother and father and siblings and interact with them. For instance, any midwife will tell you that if one baby starts to cry, all the babies in the ward will start. It seems that this response is reflecting an embryonic capacity in the newborn baby to be moved by another who is communicating in the same language of distress. An example, I was on holiday with two grand-daughters of four years old and eight months old. The four-year-old fell down and started to cry, her eight-month-old sister instantly started to cry and did not stop until her sister had recovered. This spontaneous reaction to the mood of those who are close in developmental age is very different to the reaction of an infant to its mother's mood. If, for instance, we consider the impact of maternal distress or depression on her infant, we can see a huge level of existential despair in the infant, as videos have only too painfully shown us (Trevarthen, 1977). This is in contrast to the response of one infant to the distress of another. It does not cause the same existential threat. These finely nuanced responses in the infant to its mother and to other babies suggest that they can differentiate accurately between people and between the moods of those whom they encounter in their early environment. In Stern's preface to "The Interpersonal World of the Infant" he writes, "When I was seven or so, I remember watching an adult try to deal with an infant of one or two years. At that moment it seemed to me so obvious what the infant was all about, but the adult seemed not to understand it at all… I knew the infant's 'language'. I was still 'bilingual' and wondered if that facility had to be lost as I grew older" (p. ix).

How does this help in understanding sibling incest? In our relationship with siblings, I am suggesting, there is a subtle mirroring or what Stern calls "self being with an other" reflection. We need this and mourn it if we lose it too soon, as in Pausanias' myth. Juliet Mitchell (2003. 2005) has given us good reason to believe that the birth of a sibling can cause an existential crisis, or what she calls "traumatic annihilation" (2005, p.165) if the older sibling believes the baby is him/herself.[3] However, I want to propose that such an existential crisis may reflect a failure of the environment to contain a conflict between the mystery, excitement and awe that accompanies any birth, and the powerful negative responses that comes about when the older sibling realises that this mysterious creature will not disappear at a wish. When the babies in the ward cry or my eight-month-old granddaughter cries when her sister cries, I do not believe they are confused about their own identity or what Stern would call their "self", though there is clearly an identification with the other in, what I have called "the language of distress". Stern pointed out, "There is no confusion between self and others in the beginning or at any other point during infancy" (p. 10). The other's pain may be felt but this does not mean a loss of self, but the beginning of empathy. Another grandchild when seeing her brother for the first time cried out with delight, "A baby for me!" The story of how she manages this "baby" comes later, but *ab initio* she is expressing a spontaneous delight in an aspect of life that brings her into contact with someone with whom she can have a new and intimate connection and from whom she will gain in her own emotional development.

I am suggesting that sibling relationships can crucially enrich the opportunity to develop what Stern calls "affect attunement" through the "self being with an other" and most importantly these relationships allow the playing out of "immature erotism" that Freud wrote about in 1907. It can be described in the familiar language of "I'll show you mine, if you show me yours." These games do not traumatise or overwhelm the siblings, unless, as Klein (1932) pointed out, they are fuelled by sadistic wishes. The mystery that there are areas of the body that offer up pleasure at a touch can be explored safely with "the other" because the other is the same size and shares the same excited curiosity. So long as dominance, power, and fear are not ruling these early explorations into gender identity, these experiences can lay down a foundation stone in the development of adult sexuality, as Klein has already suggested.

In order to understand why Mr D's relationship with his sister extended itself beyond the "immature erotism" of early childhood into sibling incest, the Pausanias' myth of Narcissus' search for his twin sister offers a good explanatory metaphor. The myth describes the loss of a reflection that is given uniquely by an "other" who is the same size but different. This sibling reflection is valuable for the growth of self-awareness and the enriching of the capacity for empathy with ones contemporaries. If the reflection has been strong enough in childhood it is given up in adolescence and is replaced by relationships with appropriate sexual partners outside the family. If a search for a lost twin persists in fantasy, this suggests that a sibling/peer relationship has lost its mooring or failed. In the case of Mr D the sibling incest occurred as a consequence of a weakness in the holding environment. This weakness burdened the sibling relationship with an emotional weight that it could not metabolise as Mr D became adolescent and needed to separate both from his parents and his sister. The healthy narcissistic reflection that siblings do give each other got distorted, as they carried the mother's hostility and the father's grief, and sibling incest occurred as a representation of an immature attack upon what Mr D called "the family system of communicating". The ultimate tragedy was that the sibling incest also expressed a deep grief at what was missing—the loss of parental thinking and the loss of free and safe play between the siblings.

This grief is well described by Virginia Woolf as she writes about her incestuous encounter with her half brother and the loss of her mother. "I can remember the feel of his hand going under my clothes, going firmly and steadily lower and lower. I remember how I hoped he would stop; how I stiffened and wriggled as his hand approached my private parts. But it did not stop. His hand explored my private parts too. I remember resenting it, disliked it—what is the word for so dumb and mixed a feeling?" (1985, p. 69). Later on in this Memoir she made a comment about the neglect she experienced from her mother. "I see now that she was living on such an *extended surface* that she had not time, nor strength to concentrate, except for a moment if one were ill or in some child's crisis, … Can I remember ever being alone with her for more than a few minutes? There was always interrupting" (1985, p. 94, italics added).

My patient, Mr D, left the therapy with an image of the red marks on his sister's face stretching into tentacles. The breaching of the sibling incest taboo, that "unnatural estrangement", had left damaging scars of shame and fears of retribution, but what lay behind this "unnatural estrangement" had been the *extended surface* of the parental environment that had left the siblings looking for something that could only be expressed in a tragically destructive act.

To summarise briefly my argument. I began with Austen, for she has helped to direct my attention to the natural and healing power of sibling relationships. I then suggested that we need to hold in mind what early Freud and Klein wrote about the important place sibling relationships play in our emotional and sexual development. However, we still need to find a structural theory for these relationships that give them an independent place in the internal world. I have suggested that if we push Stern's work and Pausanias' myth a bit further we might begin to have some ideas about the healthy narcissistic reflection that siblings do give each other and not least the immature erotic attachments that manifest themselves in erotic play and can later lead into creative adult erotic life. With these thoughts in mind I have attributed the breakdown of the sibling relationship into sibling incest, between Mr D and his sister, as linked to a failure in the healthy narcissistic mirroring and this was linked to a holding environment that was too "extended". In this one case the weakened family environment failed to help the children manage two necessary separations, the oedipal separation from the parents, and the sibling separation from each other.

References

Austen, J. (1814). *Mansfield Park*. London: Penguin Books (1966).

Bank, S. P. & Kahn, M. D. (1980). *The Sibling Bond*. New York: Basic Books.

Colonna, A. B. & Newman, L. M. (1983). The psychoanalytic literature on siblings. *Psychoanalytic Study of the Child*. *38*. 285–309.

Cornant-Janin, M. (2005). Incest; the crushed fantasy. In: G. Ambrosia (Ed.) *On Incest; Psychoanalytic Perspectives.* London: Karnac Books.
Faimberg, H. (2005). *The Telescoping of Generations.* New Library of Psychoanalysis. London & New York: Routledge.
Freud, S. (1907a). *Delusions & Dreams in Jensen's "Gradiva".* S.E. 9.
Freud, S. (1912d). *On the Universal Tendency to Debasement in the Sphere of Love.* S.E. 11.
Freud, S. (1915c). *Instincts and their Vicissitudes.* S.E. 14.
Freud, S. (1918b). *From the History of an Infantile Neurosis.* S.E. 17.
Forward, S. & Buck, C. (1978). *Betrayal of Innocence.* London: Penguin Books.
Herman, J. (1992). *Trauma & Recovery.* New York: Basic Books.
Hudson, G. A. (1999). *Sibling Love & Incest in Jane Austen's Fiction.* London: Macmillan Press Ltd.
Klein, M. (1932). *Psychoanalysis of Children.* New York: Delta Books [1975].
Kohut, H. (1986). Forms and transformations of narcissism. In: Morrison (Ed.), *The Essential Papers on Narcissism.* New York: University Press.
Lewin, V. (2004). *The Twin in the Transference.* London: Whurr.
Mitchell J. (2003). *Siblings: Sex & Violence.* London: Polity Press.
Mitchell, J. (2005). Sibling trauma; a theoretical consideration. In: Prophecy Coles (Ed.), *Sibling Relationships.* London: Karnac Books.
NSPCC (2000). *Child Maltreatment in the United Kingdom.*
Stern, D. N. (1985). *The Interpersonal World of the Child: A View from Psychoanalysis and Developmental Psychology.* New York: Basic Books.
Tesone, J. E. (2005). Incest(s); the negation of otherness. In: G. Ambrosia (Ed.), *On Incest: Psychoanalytic Perspectives.* London: Karnac Books.
Trevarthen, C. (1977). Descriptive Analyses of Infant Communicative Behaviour. In: H. R. Schaffer (Ed.), *Studies in Mother–Infant Interaction.* New York: Academic Press.
Volkan, V. D. & Ast, G. (1997). *Siblings in the Unconscious and Psychopathology.* New York: International University Press.
Waterhouse, L. & Stevenson, O. (Eds.) (1993). *Child Abuse & Child Abusers.* London: Jessica Kingsley.
Woolf, V. (1985.) A sketch from the past. In: J. Shulkind (Ed.), *Moments of Being.* Unpublished Autobiographical Writing (p. 83). London: Hogarth.
Woolf, V. (1927.) *To the Lighthouse.* [Reprinted: Oxford: Oxford World Classics 2006].

Notes

1. "So it was like that, James thought, the Lighthouse one had seen across the bay all these years; it was a stark tower on a bare rock. It satisfied him. It confirmed some obscure feeling of his about his own character" (Virginia Woolf, 1927, *To the Lighthouse*, p. 165).
2. Hudson (1999) in her book, *Sibling Love & Incest in Jane Austen's Fiction* explores the incest motive in *Mansfield Park*, *Emma* and *Sense and Sensibility*. I think the sliding together of "Sibling Love & Incest" in the title confuses another psychological argument in Jane Austen. Austen is suggesting early sibling attachments are never outlived; they inform and are repeated in subsequent adult sexual relationships and are the foundation stones of a good marriage. She believes that the internal model for a moral and socially constructive life is built upon the experience of relationships that "children of the same family, the same blood, with the same first associations and habits create and which no subsequent connections can supply".
3. Mitchell (2003.) has produced a theory about the essential nature of sibling relationships that goes a long way to help us understand some of the more intractable pathologies such as hysteria, Don Juanism, eating disorders, and gang warfare etc. Our neglect of the trauma that surrounds the birth of a sibling, Mitchell suggests, has meant that we do not have a sufficient psychological explanation of these, what might be called "displacement" pathologies. Mitchell's theory gives room for a lateral life that is compounded by existential anxieties about selfhood. Indeed, she suggests that this anxiety is the essential threat that the lateral life imposes. In our siblings we see ourselves and we believe they can take our place and annihilate us. It is this knowledge that is repressed and displaced in the pathologies that Mitchell discusses.

CONFERENCE 3

CHAPTER SEVEN

Developing a sense of identity as an individual

Jeanne Magagna

> She felt she was no one but a shadow of her twin.
> *"With an ancient terror, unburied in her heart."*
> Pessoa (1917, p. 25)

Introduction

Nearly everyone has a wish to have an identical twin, a "soulmate" with whom one can have an intimate communion of experiences and understanding. Being an identical twin can in some ways fulfil such a wish towards twinning, but it can also bring the fear of being but a shadow of one's twin. As a twin, there is a risk of making one's primary attachment figure the other twin. Such an occurrence can augment many problematic developmental issues, particularly those linked with avoiding the frustrations of separation. These frustrations including possessiveness, rage, and anxiety inevitably accompany a child's healthy dependence on the parents for attention, love, and companionship. Not working through the frustrations of dependence and separation in early life brings a series of problems in adolescence. This chapter will address some of the complexities of psychotherapy with an identical twin. In particular, it will examine a twin's difficulty in making full use of psychotherapy while so much of what is herself is located in the other twin and the other twin is used to defend against looking at her own most painful personal issues (Lewin, 2004). Ultimately, the chapter will illustrate how a therapeutic relationship can enable a twin to transform her identity as an identical twin into that of being a unique, separate person.

Psychoanalytic psychotherapy with one young person, Hanna, a 17 year old identical twin, will serve to show some of the complexities of helping a twin develop a sense of her own unique identity. Family therapy and group therapy supported the individual psychotherapy. Hanna, a 17-year-old American, Jewish girl, lives with her family in Cambridge where her father is working as a visiting physics professor. Hanna is about 5 foot 3 inches tall, with long, dark curly hair and dark brown eyes. She has an identical twin sister, Sarah, and a 22-year-old brother, Joseph, currently studying International Relations in the United States.

At the time of the referral

Hanna felt herself to be a twin, and nothing more. A detailed history of her life revealed that she was born prematurely and remained for six weeks in a Special Care Baby Unit. Her mother was unwell for some time and visited her on only a few occasions during the first week. When Hanna finally was brought home from hospital she cried profusely for days. Finally, she was comforted by feeding at the breast and enjoyed this experience of closeness with her depressed mother. The weaning from the breast was sudden at six months when mother's milk disappeared. At this time Hanna was inconsolable and refused to eat or drink for four days. Finally, she agreed to drink bottled milk, but only if she was fed by her father.

The parents described Hanna, who was a prize-winning ice-skater, as being accident-prone throughout her life. At her name-giving ceremony she slipped out of her mother's arms, but her father caught her and prevented her from falling to the floor. At four she fell off a trampoline and had to have her head glued. At six she fell out of a tree near the Synagogue and needed stitches on her arm. At 17 she fainted from starvation and was diagnosed as being anorectic.

What was striking throughout the stories of Hanna's childhood was that she rarely cried after the weaning at six months. She spoke in complete sentences at 17 months and seemed to be precociously talented in working the television, video and other household appliances. In contrast to Hanna's calm and collected exterior, Hanna's mother seemed to be frequently tearful or liable to angry outbursts.

Although Hanna said she was unhappy her entire life, the parents noticed her difficulties only when Hanna was 17 and her 22-year-old brother, Joseph, went to the United States for his university studies. Hanna felt her mother mourning his absence and being intensely jealous of his capturing her mother's affection, Hanna refused to write or speak to him. Three months after his departure she developed anorexia nervosa.

I doubted Hanna was really unique to the family since the mother always dressed her in red to be sure she could differentiate her from her identical looking sister whom she dressed in green. The parents felt that the twins, Hanna and Sarah, were absolutely identical in size, shape, and facial features.

I feared that when Hanna looked to her mother for an image of herself, she introjected her mother's perception of her as inextricably linked with her twin, Sarah. It felt to Hanna as though she and Sarah were part of a single being called "the twins". Certainly Hanna did not feel she was unique. In fact, as they grew older, Hanna felt herself to be the reverse side of her sister Sarah. According to Hanna, Sarah was bright, Hanna was stupid; Sarah was good, Hanna was evil; Sarah was popular, Hanna was lonely and isolated. Together, Hanna and Sarah formed a whole person comprised of good and bad qualities. Separately, they each held projections for the other. Hanna held the characteristics of being stupid, selfish, trouble-making, and lonely, while Sarah held the projections of being intelligent, kind, and likeable. In the course of their development, it is probable that Hanna introjected Sarah, but when Hanna consciously or unconsciously jealously attacked and competed with Sarah, Sarah became a damaged internal figure and thus became internalized as a damaged and weakened internalized sibling. Hanna seemed to have identified with the weakened, damaged part of the twinship. In this way rivalry between the healthy twin, Sarah, and the weakened twin, Hanna, was intensified. Such projection of aspects of the self both weakened and created limitations on the development of Hanna's personality and separate sense of self. (Dominguez and Magagna, chapter 3 of this publication). I also sensed that the destructive, belittling, bullying part of Hanna was comprised of this virulent split-off, bad part of the damaged twinship.

Through a therapeutic relationship with Hanna, I hoped both to understand the creation of Hanna's sense of being "the evil, left out" and "thick twin", and help Hanna both recover and discover a range of emotions, including both her loving and destructive feelings. This would enable her to be more than an evil, left out second twin.

What I learned from Hanna's history was that she froze rather than cried in the incubator, at six months rejected her mother for four days rather than suffer the loss of the breast, stopped speaking to her brother rather than suffer his absence when he went to university. I saw a recurrence of such detachment, freezing of feeling and rejection when for four months Hanna totally refused to either see or speak on the telephone to any members of her family. It was evident in these situations that Hanna lacked sufficient capacity to bear her experiences of separation, loss, rage, and disappointment.

Initial encounters

Hanna was admitted to a paediatric hospital in a severely emaciated state. She was 10 kilograms underweight and refused to eat. She, therefore, initially had a nasogastric feeding tube. She had a series of self-inflicted wounds on hidden areas of her legs and sides. The nurses described Hanna as depressed and withdrawn. They also said that she had low self-esteem, self-directed hostility, obsessional, and rigid behaviours. She vomited out her food and exercised strenuously for she was terrified of getting fatter. Throughout most of her admission Hanna had a delusion of being fat. At first, though, it was hard to know much about Hanna for she was virtually mute apart from the times she said, "I don't want to live. There is no point in living."

Hanna was blamed by her family for having anorexia and making it impossible for mother to complete her anthropology doctorate. Mother felt that the twins hostilely rejected her. She also felt overwhelmed by marital conflicts and the emotional burden of having adolescents who excluded her from their thoughts and activities. Father seemed absorbed in his work as a physicist. Sarah and Hanna were extremely rivalrous in their studies and friendships, with Sarah being viewed as the more successful of the two. Sarah's social life included sleepovers, wild parties with alcohol and a series of boyfriends. Hanna felt developmentally unready or uninterested in joining Sarah in her adolescent activities, but she also felt unable to live apart from her sister. Their attachment and mutual projective identification processes left Hanna desolate. She could not bear to exist without continued close intimacy with her sister. They had been functioning as mothers to each other and now, aged 17, the pressures and changes of adolescence and exams resulted in a severe disruption in their mutual support and rapport with one another.

Theoretical issues

While describing Hanna's development of a sense of self in psychotherapy I shall focus on three main issues:

1. *Transformation of the individual personality* through the use of projective identification in individual psychotherapy
2. *Twinning as a factor complicating the transformative possibilities* inherent in the therapeutic use of the transference and countertransference.
3. *Transformation of the family dynamics* through the family therapy, as an essential as an accompaniment to individual psychotherapy with an anorectic twin.

1. *Transformation of the individual personality through the use of projective identification in individual psychotherapy*

No place to go

In this first phase of therapy Hanna does not look up when I greet her for the session. After she reluctantly walks into the therapy room, Hanna sits on the couch in a foetal position, with her head hidden in the cradle of her arms. Her overflowing dark brown hair and curled up legs conceal most of the rest of her body. She feels like ice, a statue, immovable and impenetrable reminding me of Emily Dickinson's poem:

> A Quartz contentment, like a stone—
> This is the Hour of Lead…
> (Dickinson, 1862, p. 341)

Despite her impenetrability, I attempt to put myself inside Hanna's sealed off body and feel what she might be feeling. My task is to understand her silent postures and accompany this mutual resonance with my thoughts.

> "I must protect myself. I must stay safe. This place feels unsafe. I don't want to be here. I don't like this space."

> "I wonder if this is how you might be feeling", I say quietly.

Meanwhile I attempt to become essentially the identical twin in the countertransference. In this first period, it feels as though there is a kind of symbiotic knowing, but not knowing, a kind of undifferentiated relationship. In order to mitigate her sense of loneliness and despair I speak fairly frequently with descriptive phrases rather than questions. I describe how she uses her arms and legs to provide a wall around her. I make it clear that I am trying to know inside myself the feeling of being an outsider. I describe her feeling that I might just be trying to intrude upon her. "*Keep out! Keep out!*" I say. She is silent at first while I talk about her eyelids concealing her eyes, her arms covering her face, her legs hiding her so that I will not know or see any aspect of her experience. I search to understand the mood in the room generated by seeing her stiff muscle tone and posture. I communicate with Hanna's unverbalized feelings. As time progresses, I understand her a little better and can think with more clarity about her experience, I feel I am becoming a mirror (Kohut, 1971) to her feelings, an "imaginary twin" (Klein, 1963) providing another place for the feelings to be known.

There occur many sessions filled with a silent curled-up Hanna. Outside the sessions she looks and feels withdrawn from human contact. The light within her seems to have gone out thus successfully conveying her sense that "life is pointless". In one of the earlier sessions I say:

> "My arms feel safe. I must protect myself with my arms round me I must look after myself by providing my own protection, by curling up with my legs covering me".

I speak as though I am Hanna and then add,

> "When I think of your being born, being in an incubator, being left all alone with no mother, no father, needing to curl up, having to use your arms and legs to protect you, to look after yourself, by yourself. The world felt so unsafe. It felt there was no one to turn to for comfort or understanding. There seemed to be no point in living. Now though I am here trying to understand you, trying to find a way of being with you."

Much of the time when I speak Hanna remains immobile. At times I say to myself, *"Hanna feels almost dead… 'like a monumental statue set in…moveless woe' "* (Barrett Browning, 1906). I say to myself, *"I feel the lifelessness, the life with no point."*

And subsequently in another session I say,

> "It wasn't always this way you know. There was a time long ago when the breast was good, it felt good to be close to the breast and be fed. Then mother took the breast away. You were famished, weak, without anything to sustain you. The bottle milk was refused. Your sister, Sarah, became your sustenance, you clung to her, and she gave you sustenance in being there with you. Now you have been pulled away from her. She has left you more to be with her friends, do what she wants to do and that is different from what you want to do. You feel ripped off, torn away, like a leaf adrift from the tree that is necessary for its sustenance and life. A leaf without life. How to go on living, separated from Sarah? That is the question. Hanna, how can I help you find the courage to live your own life? This is the question we must answer through our work together."

I am to be present to experience the problems of a ruptured twinship, now that Hanna and her twin, Sarah, find themselves separated by two very different ways of being 17, for Hanna is afraid to join the fast-crowd with whom her sister has become friends. I wonder if Hanna's anorexia is a regressive attempt to avoid the pain of separateness from her twin, the pain of envy of Sarah's academic success and the pain of losing in their rivalrous competition in ice-skating, school, and making friends.

For most of three months Hanna is silent while I speak with her. After this she opens the fortress of her legs and places her feet on the floor. She is still protected by the cradle of her arms and a veil of overflowing long brown curly hair. Some barely audible "uh-hums" suggest agreement with a few of my descriptions of how she seems to be with others on the ward, in the sessions, in her life. I am offering my reflections as an opportunity for Hanna to begin to internalize my thinking, holding presence. I am hoping that gradually this will enable her to hold her feelings alive sufficiently long to think about them herself. It seems essential that I do not have an expectation that Hanna answer questions. What seems important is that Hanna feels nourished by my trying to understand how she is feeling in my presence. I hope that my capacity to be present for her will enable her to feel she receives enough from me to feel inspired to be more obviously present through silently thinking alongside me.

At one point I comment:

> "Your feet do bring you to the session. This makes me wonder if there is something inside you that feels you can come here, maybe a need to come here."

After three months Hanna begins speaking, but her words are spoken in such a quiet rapidly fired sequence that I feel as though I am chasing a terrified creature running away from me. It is virtually impossible to comprehend her. At other times Hanna's arms change position so that I see a silent stream of weeping tears. In one session Hanna says:

> "I just want to die. Nothing will ever be any better. I don't want to be here. I would like to run away, but I have no where to go."

The words are mumbled and inaudible, as though, like her body, her voice has lost its vitality. I have to keep asking Hanna to repeat the words. When Hanna finally locates a wish to speak loud enough for her words to reach me, she repeats variations of her statement:

> "There is no point in living, life is pointless, it will never change, nothing will ever be any good. I would like to die, life is pointless."

Then Hanna begins weeping. As on other occasions, the tears quietly flow down her face and she does not reach for a tissue. This time I decide that it is important for Hanna to realize that I am different from the incubator walls that enclosed her cries but did not comfort her. I wait for a few moments and then offer her tissues. She waits motionless for a while and then hesitatingly extends her hand to take a tissue and hold it pressed against her eyes.

Subsequently Hanna declares to both me and the nurses:

> "I don't want to do anything. I don't want to eat. I don't want to go to school. I don't want to live. What is the point? There is no point."

During this first six months Hanna complies with the rule about sitting down and eating the meals, but she neither loses nor gains weight. It takes us a long time to discover that afterwards she very secretly vomits out her meals. Hanna is also secretly self-harming, scratching hidden parts of her upper legs and waist, because she doesn't like herself, her "fat body", her life. It turns out that every couple of weeks, for six years, she has been secretly self-harming, through cutting herself. Hanna self-harmed was when she was 11 and accepted rather than defended herself against teachers wrongly criticized her at school for stealing something that her sister had stolen. When I bring up the cutting of herself in the session, Hanna says,

> "When I cut my skin it hurts. Then I can think of the pain. Thinking of the pain is the longest relief I can get from my torturing thoughts of life being pointless. I don't have to think the thoughts…just suffer the pain. The razors were with me before you."

Much of the time, though, she doesn't feel much. I understand this when Hanna describes why she refuses to see her family for four months following her admission to the paediatric hospital:

> "When my parents come to the unit I feel numb. I don't feel they are my parents. Seeing them leaves me feeling false."

I reply,

> "Maybe you are afraid to get your hopes raised if someone is important to you. Maybe you are worried that if someone is important to you, you will simply be disappointed."

Hanna replies,

> "Nobody has ever thought about me. Nobody ever thinks about me."

She cries profusely. I say,

> "Maybe you have to cry and have your cries known by me."

Hanna's tears pour down her face even more profusely. At the end of the session Hanna doesn't want to leave. I say,

> "You want me to stay with you and hear your cries, not leave you alone with them."

Through her silence and then her crying Hanna is pursuing a sense of merging into oneness with me. As I experience Hanna's tears flow into my being, I know it is important for me to be silent for a few moments while I receive them.

I am aware that Hanna had no mother present with her most of the first six weeks of her life. Her early terror of death and fears of disintegration were defended against by adhering to primitive protections, which included plastic walls, shiny metallic surfaces and the sameness of the sounds of buzzing hospital equipment.

As she cries, Hanna needs me to receive and bear the brunt of her rage, her loneliness, and her despair. Then her howl, her rage, and her cruel fury emerge with a fiery intensity. Underneath is the terror of the screaming baby wrenched from the safety of the incubator and taken home to cry non-stop for six days. But now it is safe to have feelings. There is someone to receive her screams. Hanna is experiencing that I, the in-patient nurses and her family are present for her. But as she begins to cry she also secretly scratches herself several times a week. She later explains that she has been doing this because she is experiencing an intolerable pain during the moments when she is not with me or the nurses.

Once, in a fit of anger, Hanna's mother told Hanna and her sister: *"I wish that I had never had you, never had twins."* I recollect mother's remark when Hanna says,

> "When I see my mother I don't feel anything. I don't know what the word 'mother' really means. You are supposed to feel something connected to it. I don't. I feel nothing."

Hanna explains that no one in her family ever says they are sorry. Without apologies and forgiveness, the icy coldness of hatred increases until it permeates Hanna's relationships. Then Hanna realizes that she feels nothing for her mother… Hanna resides in a freezing prison of loneliness.

Somehow Hanna never felt contained by mother internally. She kept falling and hurting herself. She had fallen out of mother's arms, out of the tree-house, onto the pavement. Mother had noticed that Hanna barely cried when she was hurt and frightened. It seems that Hanna's silence has been occurring for all her life because she does not have a sense of either an internal or external mother to whom she feels she can turn to and cry and have her cries accepted.

For all these years Hanna has held herself together emotionally through numbing her heart. Hanna's needs both in the incubator and outside at home went unmet in various ways. The muscular rigidity with which she holds herself together has been used as another primitive protection to cope with terrifying infantile fears of annihilation, of falling to pieces, of melting, of dissolving. I experience Hanna's closed off expression and curled up body and say to myself "*She feels like ice*." During these moments I suspect I am feeling Hanna's hard rigid muscularity used as a "second skin" (Bick, 1968).

Psychobiological aspects of transformation through projective identification

In the psychotherapy sessions I use an adult capacity for reverie as defined by Bion (1962). This involves providing a spaciousness of mind, a state of multidimensional receptivity to the moment-to-moment experience including what exists in my embodied presence.

Henri Rey (1994) says it is essential for the psychotherapist to arrive at the body-self if one wanted to achieve deep and enduring transformation of the patient. Alan Schore (2002) adds that the therapist's own bodily sensations in the transference-countertransference relationship are needed to provide a deepening of empathic connection with the patient. Lewis (1992) points out that the therapist's use of his/her body is especially involved in the reception of right-to-right brain transferential projections of split-off part of the self and this mechanism specifically mediates defensive projective identification. And Schore agrees that in order to transform the patient's distress, the therapist must "go beyond mirroring". More than the clinician's verbalizations, it is his or her non-verbal activity, the physical containment by the therapist of the patient's disavowed experience that needs to precede verbal processing (Dosamantes, 2002, p. 362). These spontaneous, emotional pre-attunements constitute a conversation between limbic systems. It is a biologically-based communication system that constitutes literally a biological unit (Buck, 1994, p. 266). The pre-attunement experiences create a safe holding environment (Hadiks, 1994) promoting transformation of the personality. In the following example, I use my bodily sensations to comprehend Hanna's experience and help put it into words.

> Before she speaks, Hanna sits with her head in her hands. I feel physically drained of life and then gradually become aware of a pervasive pain in my face. It is as though I have been battered. I describe how Hanna looks like all the life has been taken out of her. After a long silence, Hanna describes being assailed by inner thoughts saying "You shouldn't talk to her, it's all useless, nothing will change. You shouldn't eat, you can't gain weight, you are horrible, you are just fat, that is all." She reports this factually with no flicker of desire to challenge these thoughts. It is I who has to struggle to come to life, to release the deadness, to feel her aggression, her pain.

Hanna and I are adjusting to each other's communications in a model of mutual reciprocal influence. In addition I attempt to provide *continuity of being* (Beebe and Lachmann, 1988, p. 15) in modulating my posture and matching Hanna's vocal contour as she cries and then speaks in a mumbled, quickly paced speech. Transformation takes place through a transitional space created by my exploring within myself Hanna's projected mental pain, hopelessness, despair, and flickerings of hope. I wonder if part of what is essential for transformation through projective identification is my seeing Hanna's facial expressions of hopelessness, despair, terror, disgust, shame, excitement, elation, and rage and her seeing my facial response rather than the ceiling, similar to incubator walls. Perhaps lying on the couch would not have been a helpful option for her! I say this because Alan Schore (2002) insists that we recognize another individual's emotional state by using our right brain to recognize facially expressed non-verbal affective expressions. Of course, there is also the possibility of Hanna and I reading the expressions of our bodies, the expressiveness and intonations of our voices, but Schore (2002, p. 19) suggests that spontaneously communicated and rapidly perceived visual and auditory cures are a central component of the non-verbal right-brain communication in the psychoanalytic process.

Although Trevarthen (1980) places more emphasis on overall attunement through various modalities, I continue to ask myself if we are we depriving our patients and ourselves of certain preverbal communications by using the tradition of the couch. Gammill (1980, p. 279) says:

> "The baby comes to see in the facial expression and the eyes of his mother certain indications of the effects of his projections: he can feel how her body and skin relate and react to his own. Thus he is witness to some of the transformations his mother makes of his primitive communication, as well as being the receiver of her responses."

Successful use of the transference-countertransference enhanced both Hanna and me. At times I am filled with the damaged, despairing part of Hanna, at other times I am also holding the healthy part striving to stay alive. Sometimes she identifies with my concern and worries about her hopeless self inside me. As she experiences her feelings they stir up buried aspects of myself, my loneliness, my wish for control to just "make things different", my hatred, my pain, and my deeper capacity to love. Ultimately *we are both transformed* by simultaneously thinking together about our emotional experiences in the present moment

My use of reverie provides the possibility of psychobiologically maximizing positive affects and mitigating negative affects. (Schore, 2002, p. 10). I need to hold on to hope inside and give voice to the possibility that there can be a transformation. Through this mutual experience in the sessions Hanna and I co-create a secure attachment bond. Only through internalising this secure emotionally containing attachment bond can Hanna make the transition to being a unique individual who can psychologically separate from her twin.

2. *Twinning as a factor complicating the transformative potential of transference-countertransference communications*

Twinning research suggests that the most important relationship for almost all twins is that between the twin and her co-twin where support and reciprocity are foremost (Branje, 2002). As mentioned before, Hanna and Sarah's twinning relationship obscured difficult developmental issues that needed to be faced. These included the problems of dependence on the mother, the problems of oedipal rivalry with the father and the problems of sibling rivalry linked with the presence of other siblings in the mother's and father's minds (Meltzer, 1973).

Hanna said:

> "No one understands what Sarah means to me. No one understands what it means to be a twin. I have always been with Sarah. Sarah understands me. Sarah thinks like me."

Although Sarah was only 17, Hanna depended on her, not her parents as her source of security. She had often been disappointed though in Sarah's lack of capacity to bear Hanna's pain and on these occasions she reverted to being a mother figure to her own anguish which she projected into Sarah. When Hanna was to celebrate her birthday without her twin she was devastated. She was in a rage and said,

> "It is impossible to celebrate my birthday without my twin, she is part of me!!!"

Sarah continued to influence and contribute to the way Hanna thought and felt about herself and her world (Wright, 2004). Hanna felt that only her twin understood her and only she understood her twin. That made it difficult to achieve any intimacy with me.

a. *Having to be a twin in the transference*

In the first phase of therapy, it seems that I needed to be an identical twin in order to be valued: I had to think the same as Hanna and feel just as she felt. She needed to feel I was attuned to her exact state of mind. A difference of views could not be tolerated, for a different point of view would be a threat to twinning in the transference.

But over time I think more deeply about the relationship. I realize that I am beginning to be experienced as different from Hanna. I am to be "the bad, unwanted twin in the twinship". It is I who suffer the feelings of rejection, the tears filled with the pain of being unheard, the sense of there being no one, nothing of any value for which I should exist.

> When I walk through the door in the morning, Hanna doesn't see me. It is really as though I am invisible. I say, "Hello." My hello falls flat to the floor. I am truly "the rejected, the unwanted one".... I wonder, am I experiencing what it is to be "the second twin who shouldn't have been born at all?"

When I am repeatedly told by Hanna,

> "You understand nothing about being a twin, only Sarah understands me," I am to feel that I am "the thick twin", the "inferior twin", the "nobody" in the relationship. I am attacked as useless and experience "low self-esteem". This occurs more particularly when Hanna tells the nurses, "Therapy is useless. I don't talk, just cry."

The whole therapy with me is rubbished:

> Hanna speaks to me about feeling imprisoned. "I don't want to talk with you. I don't want friends. I don't have any friends. I have never had any friends."

Hanna is hard, angry, then soft and miserable, crying a lot. She says,

> "I have never had any real friends. I have known people who stabbed me in the back. I can't trust friends now."

But then another discourse occurs.
Hanna says softly,

> "I am worried that if I try to make a friend that Sarah will just get jealous and she won't let me have them."

Separation from her twin Sarah both socially before her inpatient admission and now during her stay in the unit, when she isn't allowed to go home, is traumatic for Hanna. Now there is a need for Hanna to individuate, to choose her own friends appropriate to her unique interests. Turning to me feels like concretely displacing Sarah to whom Hanna has been desperately clinging for survival.

But there is more involved in this twinship which frequently functions as a place to locate some of Hanna's feelings just at the moment when they get too intense and too painful, rather than bringing them into an intimate relationship. She does this by switching to saying, "Sarah is miserable, she hates my mother." Her twin Sarah might have being having difficulty with Hanna being separate, but Hanna has also projected into Sarah her own omnipotent, destructive self, defensively acting against intimacy outside the twinship. Hanna holds onto achievement rather than interdependency as a means of survival as she says:

> "The only way I can feel good in life is through getting A-stars like my sister. There is no point in having friends. I don't want friends. All I want is to be good at something. That is all I want!"

On another occasion she says:

> "If I see my mother again, I will lose my sister's love and friendship."

And later she adds:

> "I feel that my entire life I have been unliked, isolated, not part of a group…the problem is with me wherever I go."

Hanna's feeling of being isolated is confirmed by a young person who says to her, *"Speaking to you is like squeezing blood out of a stone."* Hanna reports this and adds,

> "She is right. When there is conflict all I can do is 'ice people out' and that's it. Then I am so lonely."

When in a subsequent session we are talking, I say:

> "You can stay in retreat doing nothing. You feel rejected, but have you thought, maybe also you are rejecting. It takes courage to think

with me, to make an effort not to take the easiest way out. I can help you find some courage to stick your neck out and try to create a life for yourself that you want."

b. *Turning from primitive protections to dependence on the mother*

> Shall I risk
> Sharing these words with you
> If I do
> You will gaze
> Into the heart of me
> And I am shy
> Of being seen…
> (P. Matthews, 1988, p. 108)

Moving from dependence on her primitive protections against anxiety and her adhesive clinging to Sarah, means taking a risk, means bearing the anxieties surrounding depending on a therapist who comes and goes during the week, during the holidays.

The next week Hanna comes and says:

> "I have been vomiting, standing, exercising, hiding my food, smearing my food on my plate so as not to eat it and gain weight. I want help to get better." She adds, "Do you realize that I would never have been able to say that before, nor talk to you so clearly?"

A month later, six months after her hospital admission, Hanna decides that she wants to gradually build up contact with her parents. She has begun speaking to her twin, Sarah. Hanna emphasizes that in the beginning she doesn't want *to see* her parents, she just wants to talk on the phone. She suggests that afterwards, if the phone conversation works out, she will see her parents for brief periods on the weekends. Hanna does agree to see her parents and she describes her experience saying, *"It was okay. I found something to do while I was with them."*

Just as my two-week Christmas holiday arrives, Hanna is beginning to get in touch with the possibility of depending on me and her parents. I wonder how Hanna feels about depending on me and then experiencing my departure. She lets me know when she determinedly says:

> "If I were really courageous I would really bloody myself. That would really be the way to get the attention of people."

She adds

> "How can I make anyone worry about me if I gain weight, if I am not ill?"

Hanna tells me that I feel so far away when she is out of the session. She fears that my mind is so similar to hers that she will slide out of my mind if she doesn't evoke extreme anxiety in me. Some of this fear of losing her grip on me is linked with the damage to me inside her. This damage of her internal me occurs through her rage about separating from me. Through her rage I become experienced internally as a "thick-skinned therapist" impervious to her needs. Hanna feels she has to screech out for help in order to break through my thick skin. Hanna ensures that she makes a penetrating impact on me through starving her already emaciated anorectic body or through making self-harm and suicide threats. She hopes that, if she threatens self-harm, thus thrusting anxiety about her safety onto me, then she will position herself in my mind permanently during the December holidays.

As a result of her threats, I am greatly concerned about the holidays, particularly because many of the reliable hospital staff members are away during the holidays. Before I leave for my two-week break I give Hanna a letter to hold onto. It says, among other things:

> "You have different aspects of yourself. On the one hand, with your adult self you are achieving, but you also have the baby feelings that have been with you forever…they express sadness that you have had from your infancy. This sadness will be there as you do things with people, but gradually perhaps you will find some of your sadness is transformed when you have some good intimate meetings and trust that someone can really think of you. I know your grudge against me is that I see you and then I go away. I will be away, but I don't forget about you. But you feel the gaps between our sessions."

When I return from the holiday Hanna is angry with me. She walks out of a session and then won't return for the next one. When the nurses ask her what the problem is she says:

"I feel really bad about myself. I have a very angry, nasty side. I am worried everyone will reject me for having it. She states she has been angry with me since the previous week." The nurses encourage her to come and talk to me. Reluctantly she does come and tells me that I feel different to her now that I have come back. She doesn't like how I am. She doesn't like feeling this extreme dislike for me."

After the Christmas holiday Hanna is less repetitiously using the omnipotent destructive part of her personality that she often projects into her twin who is "against therapy". Hanna is becoming more dependent on me, but accompanying this dependence is anger about being overlooked and about not having her specific needs as an individual being taken into account. When I explore her anger, Hanna I says that it is very uncomfortable to be with me because I have become a bit like a stranger to her. I wonder if her anger somehow spoils how I might feel towards her. Hanna says before she thought I liked her, but now she feels I don't like her. She does begin to see how because she doesn't like me it feels like the dislike boomerangs and I don't like her. Hanna can't imagine that I can bear being disliked by her and not return her dislike. There is no experience of a containing therapist.

Later I introduce another topic by saying,

"Maybe you could take some responsibility by initiating talking in the sessions. Maybe you could take responsibility for how difficult it is between the sessions by asking for help from the nurses outside the sessions. And later maybe rather than expecting me to understand without your speaking, you could try to put the conflicts into words, try to be honest with me about them. That would be a way of fighting the cloud of despair."

Subsequently when Hanna and I converse she says:

"No one likes me, no one will ever like me. I have spoiled my life now forever. I am bound to be a failure."

I respond,

"The cloud of despair descends, stops you from even trying to make a friend, stops you from having some good intentions to make a good life for yourself. Together we must struggle with this cloud

> of despair that hides all possibilities for having a friend, for trying to have a good life for yourself. I need you to help me by noticing how this cloud of despair accompanies every courageous thought you have."

Gradually Hanna's anorectic use of omnipotent destructiveness against dependency and intimacy lessen. Hanna's increased capacity to acknowledge her feelings and think about them with me serves to diminish the frequency of her feeling fat and fearing fatness. However, Hanna then reveals that she secretly uses obsessional rituals which include the following:

1. keeping a rigid morning routine of getting ready for school;
2. placing her serviette and spoon in a special position on the table before she can begin eating breakfast;
3. washing the parts of her body in a particular way so that the right side and left side have successive turns at being washed as she ascends up her body with the wash cloth;
4. objects have to be evenly placed balancing the same number of objects on each side of centre.

Hanna holds onto obsessional sameness of routine as a kind of "second skin" (Bick, 1968). It provides a way of holding herself together emotionally. She talks about how the slightest change in her meal plan, in her routine of rituals creates enormous anxiety. Hanna describes how it is terrifying to feel herself making this transition from perpetually feeling hopeless despair to feeling hopeful. She is afraid of being disappointed if she is hopeful and tries to work towards having something more in her life.

Hanna begins to alternate crying with talking to me. On one occasion she offers:

> "I feel you understand me. You help me get to know myself better."

Immediately, though, Hanna becomes very anxious and withdrawn. After several weeks of exploration as to why this has happened Hanna embarrassedly queries,

> "When I leave this place will you let me continue outpatient psychotherapy with you?"

Hanna experiences severe anxieties about dependence and separation the instant she experiences a growing dependence on the therapy with me. It is so frightening to count on someone other than her twin. Finally Hanna succeeds in persuading her parents and the hospital staff that she needs continuity in her therapy. It is only after we are able to finalize an agreement for outpatient psychotherapy that Hanna initiates working with me in an overtly more co-operative, responsible way.

c. *From dependence to having a separate identity*

> "She moves
> Beyond all
> Fear
> That …she will be unloved.
> And love is emerging
> So that she can be wide open to another,
> Feeling total
> Vulnerability".
> (An exchange can occur between us on many levels.)
> "Love then is a form of work
> Of courage."
> (E. Randall, 1988, p. 144)

Hanna's excitement of experiencing inner transformation is accom panied by attempts to make concrete external changes. Her clinging to the protection of thinking about calories, weight-loss and the fear of fatness, decrease significantly. Hanna is able to allow her weight to become normal for her age and height and she soon begins to menstruate.

Then one day Hanna arrives in new clothes. Several weeks later, she removes the tight clips and bands holding together her two clumps of long dark brown curly hair. Then she has her hair evenly cropped to two inches in length. At first glance I am startled into thinking,

> "She wants to be masculine. That is how she feels she can be different!"

I discover I am wrong for after a few moments of silence, Hanna embarrassedly tells me:

> "I want to be pretty, well at least as pretty as I can be. I had wanted to buy a mini-skirt but I didn't have time to get it after my haircut."

Although we first discuss Hanna's wish for external prettiness, I subsequently add,

> "Internal qualities can lead to a sense of prettiness, a sense of beauty. I wonder what internal qualities are important to you?"

Hanna responds

> "I have a biting tongue. I speak my mind too critically and it spoils my relationships. It has spoiled things with my mother and sometimes it has spoiled things with you. I want to find another way of being with people."

Hanna does indeed have "a biting tongue"! Her family and I have experienced it many times. For example, in order to feel herself a part of her peer-group, she laughs contemptuously at the nurses saying, "*They are never here to support you. They don't care. They don't understand. They are too busy.*" In part these hostile statements seem to be grievances in her relationship with me, but they are split off and projected into her relationship with the nurses. But now is an important time for Hanna is acknowledging her "biting tongue" and thinking with me about how being more caring towards me and others might leave her with the sense of internal prettiness, the sense of beauty that she desires.

Forgiving the parents

There is much work to do for:

> "Won't there be, at last,
> For the things that are
> Not death, but rather
> Another kind of ending,
> ...Something
> A bit like pardon"
> (Pessoa, 1934, p. 59)

What seems important now is that Hanna is beginning to realise how damaging her hate is and in doing so finds herself to move towards feeling less hateful and more forgiving to all of us who haven't given her exactly what she needs. As a result, she is beginning to take responsibility for using "her biting tongue". I experience her genuinely wanting to repair some of the damage done to her relationship with me, her parents, and the hospital staff.

Little by little Hanna relinquishes her grip on obsessive control to stabilize her. She is more open and vulnerable to others. Without the protection of obsessive rituals and anorectic defensive thinking, Hanna is able to acknowledge both physical hunger and emotional longings. With our help she is able to feed her hungry self. Hanna is thus beginning to emerge with a self that is surprising to see. The tense, rigid person, with mumbled words and an icy expression whom I first met seems more relaxed, warmer, with a sense of humour and an astonishingly clear, articulate way of expressing herself. Hanna has lived so many years with her infantile self carefully hidden, in exile under obsessional thinking. Now, as she welcomes her vulnerable self back into consciousness and feels something more than hate, Hanna has the possibility of entering relationships with family, friends, and society.

After nine months of individual psychotherapy Hanna's immense despair, hopelessness and loneliness is beginning to be transformed. Glimmers of hope are reflected in her witty humour as well as in her discussions about studying to be a geneticist. She wishes to have her own friends and finds moments of pleasure in being with her parents. *"I need to talk to my mother and father,"* she says. In particular, Hanna's despair has been transformed into hopefulness that psychotherapy can facilitate her passage into a life with a point to it.

Finding and keeping "her own voice" at the time of separating from the hospital unit

Hanna gradually begins to envisage leaving the paediatric hospital unit. She is recognized by her hospital peers as being a leader who "speaks her mind" and "says it as it is". She is also recognized for her dry sense of humour. Two months before she leaves the unit Hanna says:

> "I have never had such a good experience in my life as I have had here."

It is very difficult for Hanna to face the pain of separating from her inpatient peer group and the hospital team. At first Hanna's way of separating from us on the long weekends is to form a twinship again and imitate Sarah's style of living. After a weekend at home Hanna seems depressed again saying:

> "I went to a party with Sarah. It was a party with all Sarah's friends. There was drink, drugs, everyone kissing. I got so drunk I can't remember one single thing. Somehow I got home and vomited it all up. I just feel so embarrassed and miserable."

I wonder if she has permission to leave the hospital and choose her own social life. I question if she has to fit in with her sister and her sister's social plans. We discuss how it feels easier just to cling to her twin sister and try to have an identical life, but this means that she vomits out all the work we have been doing together to think about her own separate life and find her own unique style of being with friends. I remark:

> "I don't feel your wish to be connected to me to be understood; the values you have thought about for your life have disappeared."

Hanna agrees. Subsequently, before leaving the unit, Hanna decides to change schools and attend a co-educational school separate from her sister. She feels she should be in a different peer group, have her own circle of friends. She acknowledges that she wants a life separate from her sister's fast-track social life. Hanna wants to go at her own developmental pace and that means being in a fundamentally different kind of social group from her sister. Hanna does go out with her sister occasionally. After one of those outings Hanna says,

> "I nursed one drink and kept thinking, what kind of friendships would I like to have?"

She also becomes interested in one of the boys whom she meets socially, but her sister flirts with him and takes him away from her.

Hanna then decides to go to the cinema by herself rather than copy her sister in going to parties and getting drunk. She accepts that she needs to find her own friends rather than clinging to her sister. She gets a cat and decides to involve herself in a Synagogue project with deprived children.

I feel Hanna has become less isolated. No longer does she remain in retreat in the "quiet room" at the end of the sessions. Instead she waits a few moments "to gather herself together" and then she joins the young people and nurses in the central area.

3. *Transformation of family dynamics, which is required when a twin participates in individual psychotherapy*

Family therapy has been essential in identifying aspects of the twin relationship and other family dynamics that could support or impede Hanna's recovery. As well as having a twin she is now dependent on me. And very importantly, at times Hanna is able to depend on her family to be there for her and help her grow both physically and psychologically. She has let go of this need for sameness, for no change, for gluing herself in an adhesive way to her twin for friendship. In this deep place within herself Hanna is losing some primitive omnipotence that fosters a feeling that she has to be in control in an obsessive way. At times in the family meetings Hanna subjects herself to the anguish of dependency on important adults and to the anguish of suffering love, hate and sorrow for all that has happened both within her and in her relationships with her family.

Family therapy is necessary to help the dysfunctional aspects of the family. The family members required support to accept and deeply understand the vulnerable dependent and hostile, rejecting part of Hanna's personality. I cannot imagine how anyone would dream of having a young person in individual psychotherapy without helping the parents be more emotionally present and dependable for the young person, a twin, who is trying to open her heart to the parents rather than simply turning to her twin.

For family therapy it is important to have a therapist who seems inquisitive, curious and careful not to take over the mentalization capacities of the parents. Hanna was able to join the family therapy after months of rejecting the family. It is the family's capacity for mentalization, his/her containing capacity, which allows a continual development and transformation of the family dynamics. I do not intend to describe the family therapy in detail, since I am not the family therapist, but rather, I am highlighting a few important aspects of the work.

Prior to Hanna's admission into the in-patient unit, her mother, Sarah and Hanna herself continually said harsh and hurtful things in their competitive battle with one another. Hanna cites her sister's move away from her to join her "socially advanced" peer group as the major reason for Hanna's anorexia requiring hospital admission. Although Sarah initiates most of the vitriolic arguments with her mother, Hanna shadows her and is noticed laughing while Sarah angers and hurts her mother. When Hanna is admitted into the paediatric hospital, Sarah becomes both depressed and more argumentative. A picture emerges of the twins being the primary attachment figures for each other. This meant that being separated was fraught with difficulties for both Hanna and Sarah. Both had to acknowledge their feelings that were split off and projected into one another.

When Hanna finally agrees to attend the family sessions, she wants to speak to her parents. She is concerned though about all her frustrations with her parents and she plaintively asks the family therapist to help the parents understand what she feels when she speaks. It is noticeable that Sarah talks to Hanna about "getting fat" in a way that incites Hanna to remain an anorectic inpatient. Sarah has changed and admits that she is very jealous of any attention that Hanna receives from their parents and, therefore, prefers for Hanna to remain in the hospital. The family therapist assists Hanna in speaking about her feelings rather than submissively letting Sarah be the spokesperson for the part of Hanna projected into her.

Together, both Sarah and Hanna are able to share their feelings that their mother is unstable and frequently shouts and makes cruel comments to them. They also begin to acknowledge how they drive mother out of their twinship in a cruel way.
Hanna says:

> "No one in this family (including her) says, 'I'm sorry.' No one forgives and no one forgets."

The frozen relationships between family members had continued in this way for years. At one point Hanna admits:

> "I have a large ball of hatred in my gut. It is connected to the way I feel about myself and how I feel towards others in the family. This hatred leaves me feeling rubbish inside. I feel worthless. I don't deserve anything."

The mother needs her husband to be more empathic with her feelings but she continually criticizes him and does not give him the experience of being loved by her. Hanna and Sarah's adolescent difficulties seem to stir up a re-enactment of mother's own unresolved arguments with her own parents. Mother diffuses her anger with her husband by engendering an argument with Sarah and Hanna. Then father identifies with the twins' positions and that makes matters worse for mother. The boundary between the parents is thus intruded into and needs to be re-established.

The focus of the family work continues with a primary emphasis on helping the couple work together and give support to one another. Secondarily each parent is supported in helping each of their twin daughters to have separate relationships with the two of them as well as sharing in a few family activities. The family therapy also focuses upon helping each of the family members to take back their own projections of difficulties and strengths. This enables Hanna to move out of the primary focus as the symptom bearer carrying everyone's hatred, conflict and anguish.

Conclusion

Hanna feels transformed. After one year of therapy and inpatient treatment in the paediatric hospital, Hanna experiences a transformation from feeling herself to be "the no good twin" to feeling herself to be a separate individual with courage to develop a life with friends and family. The process of transformation occurs through the internalisation of parents capable of mentalising with regard to her emotional experiences. When she leaves the hospital Hanna says that she still has difficulty putting what she feels into words. She also still feels herself "to be quite fractured inside", nevertheless therapy has helped her to feel less overwhelmed by a profound despair that her entire life is "spoiled". Individual psychotherapy accompanied by family therapy and good inpatient nursing care enable Hanna to see the possibility of a future for herself.

Now we continue the outpatient psychotherapy while Hanna is living away from home to pursue her university studies. There is so much more work to do! Hanna still has a fragile sense of self, but the psychotherapy sessions provide a space for the icy split-off self to melt to tears...tears representing longing, fear, anger and love. Within this space for reverie Hanna is sometimes able to locate in her heart a place to give birth to words that lift her feelings into more discrete and knowable entities. In verbally sharing her experience "a whole hidden life comes flooding back to consciousness" (Malouf, 1999). Slowly, painfully, she allows her feelings to be reintegrated back into herself. She is finding her unique, individual self.

Life within her family is still very strained, but Hanna has been able to have a life away from her twin and family. At times of particularly intense difficulty she retreats to using her twin as the receptacle for her anguish and struggles to maintain her weight. Despite these continual struggles Hanna is able to feel enthusiastic about her university studies and has developed some close friendships with young people of both sexes. Life is still fraught with enormous difficulties and fears of being a responsible young adult. The "cloud of despair" still hovers around at times. Despite all this, I feel Hanna "straining forward to whatever life it is that lies out there beyond our moments together" (Malouf, 1999).

References

Barrett Browning, E. (1906). *Grief. The Poetical Works of Elizabeth Barrett Browning.* London: Smith, Elder, & Co.

Beebe, B. and Lachman, F. M. (1988). The contributions of mother-infant mutual influence to the origin of self and object representation. *Psychoanalytic Psychology* 5(4): 305–337.

Bick, E. (1968). The experience of skin in early object relations. *International Journal of Psychoanalysis,* 49: 484–486.

Bion, W. (1962). *Learning from Experience.* London: Heineman.

Branje, S. J. T. (2002). Relational support in families with adolescents. *Journal of Family Psychology 17*: 445–459.

Buck, R. (1994) The neuropsychology of communication: spontaneous and symbolic aspects. *Journal of Pragmatics, 22*: 265–278.

Dickinson, E. (1862). After great pain. In: T. H. Johnson (1964) *The Complete Poems of Emily Dickinson.* New York: Little, Brown and Company.

Dominguez, G. and Magagna, J. (2009) In this book Ed. by Lewin and Sharp, Chapter 3.

Dosamandes, I. (1992). The intersubjective relationship between therapist and patient: a key to understanding denied and denigrated aspects of the patient's self. *The Arts and Psychotherapy, 19*: 359–365.

Gammill, J. (1980). Some reflections on analytic listening and the dream screen. *International Journal of Psychoanalysis, 61*(3): 375-381.

Hadiks, D. (1994). Nonverbal aspects of therapist attunement. *Journal of Clinical Psychology, 50*: 393-405.

Klein, M. (1963). On the sense of loneliness. In: *Envy and Gratitude and Other Works.* Reprinted1980. London: Hogarth Press (pp. 300–313).

Kohut, H. (1971).*The Analysis of the Self.* New York: International Universities Press.

Lewin, V. (2004). *The Twin in the Transference.* London and Philadelphia: Whurr.

Lewis, P. P. (1992). The creative arts in transference/countertransference relationships. *The Arts in Psychotherapy, 19*: 317–333.

Malouf, D. (1999). *An Imaginary Life.* London: Vintage Press.

Matthews, P. (1988). Where beauty lies. In: *Transformation: The Poetry of Spiritual Consciousness,* J Ramsay (Ed.). London: Rivelin Graphen.

Meltzer, D. (1973). *Sexual States of Mind.* Perthshire, Scotland: Clunie Press.

Pessoa, F. (1917). In *The Surprise of Being.* Translated by Greene, J and de Azevedo Mafra, C. (1986). London: Angel Books.

Pessoa, F. (1934) In *The Surprise of Being.* Translated by Greene, J. and de Azevedo Mafra, C. (1986). London: Angel Books.

Randall, E. (1988). Beyond all other. In: *Transformation: The Poetry of Spiritual Consciousness.* J. Ramsay (Ed.). London: Rivelin Graphen.

Rey, H. (1994) Anorexia nervosa In: J. Magagna (Ed.), *Universals of Psychoanalysis.*

Schore, A. (2002). Implications of a Psychoneurobioloigcal Model. In: S. Alhanati (Ed.), *Primitive Mental States Volume II.* New York: Karnac Books.

Trevarthan, C. (1980). The foundations of intersubjectivity: development of interpersonal and co-operative understanding in infants. In: D. R. Olson (Ed.), *Before speech: The beginning of interpersonal communication.* New York: Cambridge University Press.

Wright, S. (2004). *Palatable Differences: An Exploration of the Development of Anorexia Nervosa within the Context of the Twin Relationship Experience.* Doctoral dissertation: University of East London.

CHAPTER EIGHT

Taking account of siblings—a view from child psychotherapy[1]

Margaret Rustin

> *Psychoanalysts have given far less attention to the fantasies and affects relating to brothers and sisters than to those concerning the parents even though siblings, whether real or imagined, are just as much a constituent of the family constellation that shapes the child's psyche.*
>
> (Houzel, 2001)

Introduction

This paper attempts to explore an area of our emotional lives which has been relatively neglected in the literature of child development, family dynamics, and psychoanalysis, although not, in my view, within child psychotherapy practice or, as Mitchell (2006) has pointed out, in the group analytic tradition. In both these contexts awareness of the importance of siblings seems inescapable. However, theoretical attention to sibling relationships in psychoanalysis has not been extensive until a more recent flurry of publications and conferences on this theme. There are probably quite complex explanations for this phenomenon and some will be suggested in this paper, but within child psychotherapy there are a number of background factors to bear in mind. These include the impact of family work and family therapy on the thinking of child psychotherapists. One might perhaps say that our frame of reference tends to extend Winnicott's dictum about the impossibility of conceiving of a baby without a mother much more widely. There can, after all, be no mother without a father, in some sense, however limited his active presence may be in the increasing numbers of one parent or alternative families (Trowell and Etchegoyan, 2002). Most certainly we encounter paternity as a fact of life in the internal world in clinical practice (Money-Kyrle, 1978). Grandparents, too, are very frequently in the frame when we take into account the inter-generational unconscious transmission of beliefs about fundamental relationships, as has been a powerful source of deeper understanding from Fraiberg's seminal work onwards (Fraiberg, 1980), particularly evident in the field of Infant Mental Health. So, too, with siblinghood. The sibling aspect of a child's identity is present obviously enough in those families where siblings are present, but I shall argue that we also have evidence that a child without brothers or sisters is concerned with their external absence and dealing with this in his inner world. The importance of imaginary siblings as a replacement for missing siblings is one thread in the world of imaginary companions, a theme recently explored in Adamo (2006).

I shall mention four other factors highlighting sibling issues for child psychotherapists. The first is the dual impact of the lengthy training process, in which peers are so vital a feature (often becoming life-long friends) and the joint work so characteristic of our practice; when one therapist sees a child and another works with the family, there is a couple at work who can perceive themselves (or be perceived) as a quasi-parental couple, but also potent is the idea of two siblings collaborating. The second is the small but creative tradition of group work within child psychotherapy. The analytic exploration of mixed children's groups (even more obviously in the case of work undertaken with sibling groups as such) always produces rich material about both conscious and unconscious aspects of sibling relationships (Canham and Emanuel, 2000). The third comes from the troubled preoccupation in the case of looked after children with the issue of whether and how to place siblings together. The evidence from long term outcome studies suggests that maintaining birth family relationships is a protective factor, although as with any generalization, such a trend in policy and practice needs to attend to the individual case which may not always be best served by general principles. In this journal, Hindle's research work on this topic is reported (2007). A fourth is the investigation of the fate of "replacement" children, when the lost sibling who remains alive and unmourned in the mind of the mother can cast a shadow that threatens the life-space of the subsequent baby. This theme has been extensively described by Reid (2003) and more recently explored in research work using participant infant observation as a methodology (Gretton, 2006).

Finally, the fact that the theoretical education of child psychotherapists is solidly rooted in the reading of the classical clinical papers of Freud and later analysts and child psychotherapists ensures a vivid awareness of sibling life. Sherwin-White's scholarly demonstration (2007) of Freud's attention and interest in sibling themes serves as an apt counterweight to the claim that siblings had to be discovered by psychoanalysts in the 21st century! The ongoing re-evaluation of the place of siblings in psychoanalytic theory (Mitchell, 2003; Coles, 2003, 2006; Lewin, 2004) is welcome, but child psychotherapists may feel some puzzlement.

The one widely accepted assumption about sibling relationships that dominates the field is the importance of sibling rivalry, an idea theorized by Freud in relation to his broader theory about emotional and sexual development. This concept leaves out the dimension of sibling love and places the emphasis firmly on hostility, destructive competition and the idea of there never being enough love to go round, an unavoidable Lacanian lack, one might say. Recent writers have begun to revisit these quite basic questions. But in our consulting rooms, it seems to me that it has always been obvious that the ambivalence (the mixture of love and hate) characteristic of other intimate relationships was also characteristic of sibling relationships. Clinical experience with children repeatedly reveals the vital significance of real, lost and imagined siblings.

Sociological factors

Before going on to present what I hope will be a recognisable picture of child psychotherapy's approach to understanding siblinghood, I want to raise another question; why might it be that sibling relationships have become a renewed source of both professional and wider public interest at this time? The press features such topics as the importance or not of birth order, the desirability or not of one-child families; the siblings of public figures become objects of interest (e.g. Lord Spencer emerged as a public figure because he was Princess Diana's brother); political clans cluster around bands of brothers (the Bush family is an example to rival the Kennedys in the U.S.); and Hollywood too is fascinated by siblings. Part of this is just the cult of celebrity, but the fact of siblinghood, the sense of the shared intimacy of childhood, does seem to be a special source of public fascination.

There are probably significant social-historical factors at work here. First there is the lifespace of late adolescence and early adulthood. At this crucial point in the life span, sibling relationships or sibling-like relationships have acquired greater centrality since the very long educational experience of our adolescents and young adults often serves to delay marriage and the choice of sexual partner seen as long-term companions. Instead of our 20–30 year olds setting up family, in the more highly educated sectors there tends to be a protracted period of living something more like an adolescent group life, a sort of extended student existence for many 30 somethings, as some of the popular sitcoms record, or sometimes a return to the parental home for the post-college young people who cannot afford independent living. This means that instead of moving from being the adolescent children of our parents into adult partnerships in which we are potential parents, there is often a protracted period in which our identity may be defined by our families of origin, including our sibling relationships.

Then there is the extended span of life in the developed world and our extraordinary geographical mobility. We are living longer than earlier generations and we are also much more itinerant and much less likely to sustain life-long partnerships. Perhaps our adult siblings are becoming more important as sources of continuity and support over a lifetime in these increasingly complex life-worlds. The death of our parents often does not take place until we are well on into our middle age, but prior to that there can be long periods of time during which their care becomes a major preoccupation. It is siblings with whom we can share the practical, emotional, and financial burdens of caring for elderly parents. This can be an important period of coming closer again or not, as the case may be. The general tendency for some reduction of social welfare provision in the Western world throws greater responsibility back onto the family where it is a functioning system, and those without such resources are at risk of marginalization. The growth of old-age communities, another modern phenomenon, may, of course, bring in sibling-like experiences for their inhabitants, since these are uni-generational communities in which one's neighbours may well be experienced as more like siblings at an unconscious level.

One final and obvious point about the wider social context is that the rate of maternal employment outside the home has enormously increased. This has at least two relevant consequences. First, mother as the primary focus for the young child's emotional life is less available. Nannies, childcare and nursery workers and babysitters become important people. Possibly this new framework for the early years may also heighten the dependence of little children on the siblings in the family. They may become the most steadily available attachment figures (to use Bowlby's term), something one sees very strongly indeed when families break down and children are taken into public care, when a child's identity can be focused intensely on membership of the sibling group. Secondly, vast numbers of young children are now in group day-care from early on in their lives. While not actual siblings, the other children in the group are undoubtedly experienced as quasi-siblings, since they share the attention offered by the day-care maternal and paternal substitutes. The evidence from large-scale studies of day-care often points to two aspects of the children's experience. The children are described as more able to engage in social play and peer relationships than family reared children, and this is valued positively as part of early education and socialisation. By contrast, it is also frequently noted that children placed before about two years of age in extensive large group day-care tend to be more aggressive and less co-operative. There is a vital debate to be had about the optimal age for entry into full-time group day-care but also a most interesting range of theoretical questions raised by this data. The point I want to underline, however, is that millions of children now grow up spending large amounts of time in a group care situation, where their feelings about the other children probably reflect variations on sibling-like themes.

The psychoanalytic contribution to theorising siblinghood

I shall turn now to the pictures of sibling relationships that psychoanalytic theory makes available to us. I want to address this not by giving a historical account of the development of theory, but rather by describing the place of siblings in the growing child's mind and linking that to the contribution of particular theorists. To address the very beginning, we need to consider the unborn infant. Here I am relying on imaginative speculation that is in line with clinical experience. Unless the foetus is part of a twin or multiple pregnancy, we might imagine that the foetus has an experience of blissful uninterrupted possession of mother's internal space. This is, however, an idealised oversimplification, since we know that the foetus has an awareness of sounds from outside mother's body (voices, music, etc.) and of disturbances from the body if mother is ill, hurt or distressed during the pregnancy, and that it experiences all kinds of variations in the flow of nutrients depending on mother's diet and lifestyle. So the idea of a wholly protected inner sanctum does not accord with the facts. Attempting any such description raises the interesting question of what level of development of mind there is pre-birth. Might the foetus have some preconception, some sort of as yet unrealised idea, of mother as potentially having other babies, or would that be restricted to those babies who have actually shared space in the uterus? In unconscious phantasy, the baby whose sojourn within mother has become uncomfortable in later pregnancy due to position, size or other factors might perhaps imagine that the pressure of the diaphragm or pelvis is evidence of the presence of rivals for space. Certainly the foetus whose mother is subjected to domestic violence might construe this external assault as evidence of hostile invasion of an inner safe place if mind has developed to the point where such a thought-in-feeling might be registered.

More obviously, once the baby is born, the baby's awareness that a transition from inside mother to outside mother has taken place does imply that the inside-mother space is now vacant and could house someone else. The growing evidence of the sophisticated mental capacities of tiny babies makes this a much less improbable hypothesis than it once seemed. Even if we do not locate the germ of this idea at birth, we can certainly see evidence in the close observation of babies a few months old of a preoccupation with what is going on inside mother's mind and body. The familiar early toddler play of emptying mother's handbag of precious contents, of the fascination with Russian doll-type toys, of the innumerable variations of containing shapes into which things can be put, attest to the young child's intense interest in a maternal space in which things can grow. Watching children's play sparks off vital questions, and the detailed observational material studied in Young Child Observation undertaken in pre-clinical courses is a rich source of conviction about the meaningfulness of play and its capacity to illuminate the inner world of the child shared by child psychotherapists (Adamo and Rustin, 2001).

It was just this sort of observation that started Melanie Klein's investigation through clinical work with very young children of the unconscious picture the child has of the fundamental relationship links of the family. What she discovered was that her young child patients showed her a very complex picture of mother's body and of mother's relationship to others in the family, both real and imagined. She proposed that this picture was constituted through the child's physical and emotional experience of maternal care. Mother was made from the baby's point of view, of feeding, holding, looking, listening, cleaning, and vocalising elements. She was sometimes there and sometimes not. The baby's initial total dependence on her meant that all experiences of babyhood contributed to the early picture of mother. Klein emphasised the relationship to mother's breast because of the centrality of the infant's feeding relationship, but she also described the baby's feeling of depositing his urine and faeces directly into mother, as if the nappy were also felt to be part of mother's body. All the elements of infant care very gradually come to cohere in the baby's mind as parts of a whole. So instead of having a lovely warm nice-milk Mummy which is not linked up with the horrible absent Mummy that the cold or hungry baby might be screaming about, there is a joining up of the features and a picture of a whole Mummy appears in the child's mind, in which the beloved aspects and the hated and disappointing features can be integrated.

The more integrated mother figure is one from whom the baby is able to feel separate. At this point the idea that some other baby might displace him becomes part of the picture. Of course, this sense of there being a space between mother and baby is enormously amplified by the actual experience of being weaned. If one is not drinking the milk in mother's breast oneself it is certainly an immediate question as to whom else might do so. Sometimes difficulties in weaning on the baby's side seem to be linked with an unconscious belief that he or she can hold onto possession and thus prevent the appearance of rival babies. Similarly, some sleeping problems are connected with an unconscious desire to prevent Mummy and Daddy having any chance to make any new babies (Daws, 1989). The terribly painful situation we have probably all observed when a young child is faced with a new baby feeding and really cannot bear it and tries to interrupt, intrude and attack either baby, mother or both, is always a vivid reminder of just how desperate things can be for the child who feels displaced from mother's lap.

The Contribution of Infant Observation

Klein's thinking about very early development has been taken further by later writers (Bick, 1968; Tustin, 1972; Houzel, 2001; Briggs, 2004) who have been greatly influenced both by naturalistic observation of infants and by work with children with early emotional difficulties. Their crucial discovery has been that the infant's sense of identity is fundamentally relational. One is *mother's* baby, at depth, and, therefore, if mother has another baby, one loses one's known position in the family and the world. The level of anxiety the displaced young child feels is, therefore, existential—a time of catastrophic change, in Bion's terms (1970).

A recent reading of a number of accounts of infant observation brought this feature vividly to life. It is striking how often infant observers find themselves observing a new baby and a confused, displaced young child, sometimes desperately struggling to hold on to his place with mother and to cope with the fact that he has become one of two. Most Infant Observation seminars find themselves with at least one such story unfolding. There is a compelling account of the dynamics involved in Cooper's chapter in "Intimate Transformations" (Magagna et al., 2005). The observer in such situations experiences the struggle going on in mother's mind to make a space for each child as she, too, feels the pull of intense identifications of each child's position. Because of the special place of the training in infant observation in British Child Psychotherapy trainings (Sternberg, 2005) this ensures that exposure to the existential importance of siblings is a core part of a child psychotherapist's state of mind. Cooper discusses the triangle of mother, toddler, and baby as potentially excluding the place of father. This idea can, however, be counterposed to the familiar fact of the quartets which emerge in many families at this time, toddler turning to father, or maybe grandmother, in the face of mother's preoccupation with the new baby. These two pairs can be a very comforting structure, either offering the pleasures of splitting-off the unwanted complexities of threesomes or providing a breathing space from the exposure to sibling rivalries and oedipal intensities.

The intergenerational element in the new mother's response to the arrival of a second or subsequent baby is also highlighted by infant observational material. In Cooper's example, she quotes mother's decision not to breast-feed baby Anna, which reversed her previous intention: "I decided to give her formula. I just couldn't do breast-feeding and look after James. I couldn't have her literally attached to me. I wouldn't be able to keep up with him." As James (18 months) furiously attempts to interrupt the baby's feed, mother remarks, "I feel so bad for him. He had me all to himself."

Cooper suggests that mother's experience of having an older brother underlay this overwhelming identification with James and made it difficult for her to shield Anna from his intrusions (Cooper, pp. 44–45). By contrast are those observations where one sees a family culture in which siblings are expected by and large to enjoy each other's company, and to see a new baby more as precious companion then deadly rival, and where there is space for the different needs of individuals. We might possibly suggest that the larger families not now so frequent in western societies give rise to a strong sense of the sibling bond as a central organizing fact of life. Briggs' fascinating account of the band of brothers of whom the little boy he observed was the youngest member is a memorable example of this (Briggs, 1997).

An everyday story and a clinical example

Nonetheless the devastating loss of security is probably an inescapable aspect of the displaced child's experience of a new baby's birth. One three-year-old responded thus. She announced that she was now the big sister, that is she believed she had to enter into a new identity at once—otherwise she would be nobody. This gave rise to great practical problems. She was not yet reliably dry at night and had been continuing to wear nappies. But big sisters don't wear nappies, she explained, and insisted she could not do so—it was babies who did that. Unfortunately for the poor parents, this big sister self couldn't actually persist through the night, so endless wet beds ensued. Feeding the new baby in the small hours would be mixed up with looking after the rejected baby-self of the three year old and the mother felt that the reality for her was that she had two babies at night time for some weeks.

A similar picture seemed to be the basis for the clinical problem I was faced with in my work with a psychotic child when I became pregnant. I had already seen this child for some years, and her treatment was planned to continue after my maternity leave. One day well on in my pregnancy she had a particularly extreme tantrum in her session, screaming loudly and desperately for a long time. When she had recovered herself, she looked at me very anxiously and explained that she was worried she had woken the baby up and that the baby would come out too soon and be angry with her (she was herself a premature baby). For weeks she begged me about "seeing the baby" after the birth. I came to believe that this was her way of asking about whether she as my patient-baby at the clinic could trust me to return to her, that is that she would go on seeing me, and this is how I interpreted to her, but I wasn't sure I was right. When my baby was born, I had arranged with my little patient's mother that she would be able to telephone me so that she could hear my voice. She said only two things after I had told her that the baby and I were both well. "Is it a girl or a boy?" (I told her it was a girl) and "What is her name?", which I told her. This conversation obviously raises large issues of technique which I cannot pursue here, but which require debate. When we resumed work some time later, she never spoke further about this actual baby of mine and instead did indeed seem to be primarily concerned about the safety of herself as the baby, that is the belief in the continuing place she had with me in treatment, that I had returned as the therapist-mother for her ill baby self. She did not seem to have hostile feelings towards my home-baby to any great extent—on the contrary, the safe arrival of a new baby seemed to give her some confidence that babies could be looked after.

Affection between siblings

This brings us to the question of positive feelings between siblings. I shall return to the three-year-old and her baby sister described earlier. What was fascinating to observe was the mutuality of passionate affection that grew between these two. The big sister regarded herself as the champion of her little sister from early on in life. For example, the arrangements for her first birthday party were a topic of enormous interest—who was to come, what the one year birthday girl would wear, where she would sit at the table, what sort of birthday cake she would have, what games and toys a one-year-old and her baby friends would like. All these were things on which the four-year-old had a lot to say, not primarily in the spirit of competition or of controlling the event, but based on identification with the baby's point of view and an effort to imagine what that might be. This sense of presiding benignly over the experiences of a younger sibling is particularly marked when new demands from the wider world impinge. Going to playgroup or nursery and later school or to the dentist or hairdresser can, of course, be occasions on which the older child can patronise, tease, and indeed torment the younger one. But just as significant is the wish to protect and comfort the beloved sibling by sharing the worry and by demonstrating that one survives quite well.

From the perspective of the younger sibling, the older one is part of the structure of the primary human environment. "Me and Poppy" was the way one small boy habitually referred to doing anything that involved himself and his older sister and it sounded pretty much like a fixed unit, a twosome that certainly rivalled in its importance the twosome of the parents. We might think of it as a sort of "we" ego. This is a very important function of siblinghood. The single child who has to share parents with a new arrival in the family does have to deal with rivalry, but at the same time gains a partner, and this mitigates the loneliness that a singleton can also experience. The sharing of what it is like to be at the centre of parental attention can also sometimes be a considerable relief. Not only does the child gain a companion, and one who will at times certainly be an ally in mischief and rebellious discontent with parental demands, as well as a playmate with whom a shared imaginary world can be created, but also it can lift a burden when one is not the only repository of the family's expectations and projections. The responsibility to please parents and grandparents, or more troublingly, for example, to cheer up a depressed mother, or protect a vulnerable parent, or witness and worry about parental quarrels or domestic violence can be very heavy.

The friendship that develops in Pullman's *The Subtle Knife* (1997) between Will and Lyra, the hero and heroine of the trilogy, is a beautifully realised initially sibling-like relationship that rescues each of them from the pressures of being an only child. Will has a mother who has lost a husband and is depressed, confused, and helpless to a psychotic degree. He has become the carer of a broken-down parent. Lyra is the child of narcissistically warring parents, simultaneously neglected, unpredictably spoilt, and wilful. In finding each other on their journeys into other worlds, which represent the growing-up process and the building of more durable internal structures based on being able to depend on and to respect other people appropriately, they recover from their difficult beginnings (Rustin and Rustin, 2003). The enrichment of the world of play and the whole life of the imagination when a child acquires a sibling is almost impossible to overestimate. The shared games, imaginary characters, secrets and adventures of childhood are remembered and referred to over a lifetime and provide a model for intimacy that informs later friendships and love relationships. There is no doubt that siblings can also sometimes make up for deficiencies in the relationships with parents through what they create with each other (Anna Freud's famous research study of a group of war orphans made this point in a situation of quasi-siblinghood (1974).

Groups and Gangs

I have been discussing the transition from one to two children in a family but, of course, often (though less so nowadays when families are smaller) there are more, and the siblings constitute a group. This creates new tensions and opportunities for psychological growth. Learning to function as a member of a group, and for the group to cope with issues of leadership, equality of and respect for its members, allowing for differences—for example of age and gender—is a large task. There is valuable psychoanalytic writing about the distinction between group life and gang life (Waddell and Williams, 1991; Canham, 2002), and it is in sibling groups that these dimensions can first be explored. Children who have had no such experience before they go to nursery have to meet the demands of group life there for the first time.

What are the essential differences between group and gang formations? By 'group' in this context is meant a collection of people with a recognisable boundary (eg. siblings, a school football team, or indeed a CAMHS [Child and Adolsecent Mental Health Service] team) whose relationships are predominantly determined by commitment both to particular values (e.g. fairness, concern to protect weaker members) and to the larger aim which is the group's raison d'être. In the case of sibling groups this larger aim includes the development of all the individuals in the group, the enrichment of the group's culture, the support of the members of the group and the encouragement of their linking to those beyond its boundaries in wider friendships and activities. By contrast, gangs exist to override the interests of individuals by subjecting them to a primitive or pathological authority working in the direction of cutting gang members off from intimacy with anyone outside, and asserting that the gang is the structure that protects its members from the hostility by which it claims to be encircled. In psychoanalytic terms, a pathological and cruel or confused and perverse superego dominates the gang in contrast to the more benign and supportive superego of what I am defining as group culture (Canham & Emanuel, 2000).

A very interesting literary example of a sibling group that deteriorated under pressure is the subject of Ian McEwan's excellent novel *The Cement Garden* (1996) from which a film was later made. It concerns a group of four siblings. Their father dies at a point when his state of mind lacks creativity and warmth, symbolised by his plan to concrete over the garden. The mother is overwhelmed, becomes ill and also dies soon afterwards. The children decide to hide the mother's dead body in order to avoid being taken into care, in other words to behave as if there were still parents around and that they could reconstitute the family on their own. The older sister has to "become" mother, and this leads to intense confusion for all of them in different ways. The narrator, the oldest boy, who is in the throes of adolescence, is filled with incestuous longings for his sister whom he cannot now distinguish from the lost and not-yet-mourned mother. There are no parents present to set limits to this, and once his jealousy is roused by the appearance of his sister's older boyfriend, incestuous *enactment* takes place. It is quite clear that an ordinarily complicated family has been catapulted into catastrophe by the intensity of painful loss, the children's unconscious guilt about the death of their parents and their desperate efforts to deny the reality, which involve ever greater isolation from the wider society. A group of ordinarily ambivalent siblings has become a deeply disturbed parody of a family in which the psychological needs of each of them are misunderstood and great damage is inflicted. This reminds us that sibling relationships necessarily imply parents in the background, whether present or not. If the link to parental figures is attacked, the nature of the sibling connection is distorted and basic differentiation undermined.

Imagined Siblings—unconscious phantasies

So far I have been discussing in the main real-life sibling experiences or their representation in literature. I now want to turn to the babies imagined to inhabit mother's mind and body. These are the babies we believe our mother is busy thinking of when not attending to us, the babies that may be born in reality and that in any case are occupying some of the inner spaces of mother's mind and body in our unconscious phantasy. Children's dreams and drawings quite often include reference to these ideas, and in psychotherapy the theme often becomes explicit. Different versions of this phantasy appear according to the child's stage of development and of course influenced by actual experience. One very early version is what Tustin referred to as "the nest of babies" phantasy (Tustin, 1972). This is an idea she found particularly prevalent in her work with autistic children and it has been developed in important work by Houzel (Houzel, 2001). The child's belief is that inside mother are a whole lot of babies, just like a nest full of baby birds all waiting to be fed. This nest is sometimes felt to be located in mother's breasts, where they are greedily drinking all the milk, but can also be located in mother's head (a mind full of noisy rivals) or mother's womb (all enjoying perpetual warmth and peace).

The developmental importance of siblings in the internal world—a clinical example

The child whose material I am drawing on demonstrated a particularly interesting link between a dawning capacity to imagine a world peopled by siblings and the concurrent development of symbolic capacity and playfulness.

Sophia is the daughter of a highly educated Moslem Arab father and a Welsh working class mother with a history of familial sexual abuse. Both parents have considerable long-term mental health difficulties. She is in weekly therapy. Her most serious problems are linked to a failure to separate from mother in any meaningful way, consequent identity confusion, and enormous difficulties in relating to other children. She frequently claims to have been bullied at school, while all the evidence points to her attempting to manipulate and control other children in the same way that she does her mother and her large collection of pets at home, and her *rage* when they object.

In her sessions with me, she at first seemed extremely disturbed, as she was unable to play and talked non-stop in a jumble of past and present, reality, fantasy, and dreams. It was almost impossible to remember the sequence of what she said as there was no apparent logic or sense of temporality. As she gradually became aware of the structure of the therapy, the regularity of her sessions, of my attempt to understand her and of my persistence in staying outside the confusional world she inhabited, a more normal side of her began to appear. She became less interested in the idea that she knew everything about the Tavistock (unfortunately this idea was nurtured by mother's boundaryless relationship to the building) and less convinced that she had seen me in all sorts of other places—on the bus, at the shops, in the park, etc. She would in fact succeed in making me feel quite unsure whether she might actually have done so, and it was eerie to feel I was perpetually under her gaze. Instead, she began to feel very curious. Were the other drawers in the chest of drawers of which she had one for her play materials used by other children? Did I live in my room at the Tavistock (after all there was a couch which might be my bed she remarked) or did I live somewhere else? Did I know J.; another child from her school who she thought came to the clinic? She began to squint out of the waiting room window and try to see into my window, which was at a right angle to it. As she left the clinic, she would gaze up at the row of windows and try to identify mine and see who might be in the room with me after her. Despite the discomforting intrusiveness of her curiosity, the situation now felt much more real, with a palpable distinction between inside and outside.

She seemed to me to be working through a move from an idea that she was in complete possession of me, representing the internalised mother in her mind, to one in which she took her place among my other children, that is the other patients she was now so interested in. As this shift took place, the play with the small animals and dolls that had developed after the initial months of verbal outpouring took a very different turn. Earlier play had focused on total oedipal confusion—the baby horse would always turn out to be marrying the mother, following some mysterious catastrophe occurring to the father horse, for example, or, less obviously, all the animals would be arranged in odd-assorted couples and the baby animals were in couples in exactly the same way as the adult ones—family groups simply did not exist, and all partnerships were perpetually dissolving and reforming. In this animal world, there were frequent wars and natural disasters so that no one seemed safe. Some order began to appear when she grew keen on the idea that an animal king and queen were in charge overall. At first, the royal couple might be an adult/child combination, but after much interpretation of her wishes not to see the differences between grown ups and children, the king and queen were represented by two grown up and matching animals, one of each sex.

Soon after this, a new game began to take shape and this game turned out to be very relevant to my theme. She arranged a school, with a nursery, reception class, grade 1, 2, 3 and 4, and a headteacher's office with a secretary who could arrange access. In each imaginary classroom that was set up in a different part of my room, the teacher was given the appropriate materials for the children. For example, tiny tissues were provided for the reception children, so that they could learn to blow their noses. A small animal was sent from the reception class to take a message to the headteacher. This was shown as a very long journey, but completed successfully, but on returning, the little animal could not manage to climb up the very last step into the classroom and was at risk of tumbling downstairs. This echoed innumerable earlier games in which animals would always be falling unnoticed to the ground from great heights, but on this occasion the teacher eventually noticed the child's struggle and helped him back in.

For Sophia, it is quite clear that there is a link between being a child kept in mind and being one of a group of children for each of whom there is a proper space. Her therapy sessions with me have helped to build a mental structure in which she can safely move out of the position of being the baby inside mother, that is not being born psychologically as a separate person but remaining terribly confused with mother. Her original presentation as the prematurely aged and overweight child of her obese mother had underlined the extent of this pathological identification. Now she can instead visualise the world as one in which there is a separate appropriate space for each child, herself and the imagined sibling group, and learning and development can take place as in her imaginary school. Not continuing to live inside mother seems to coincide with the recognition that she is *one* of the children, not the one and only one. I anticipate that this will gradually enable her to make friends in a more ordinary way with other children. She has weathered psychological birth.

Lost siblings

There is one more theme I want to touch on, and that is the impact on a child of the death of siblings. The most frequent situation in which this becomes a vital matter is when there are maternal miscarriages either before or after a child's birth. Considerable clinical research work has and is being undertaken on this theme of the "replacement" baby (Reid, 2003) and it elaborates the risk to the child who is born following late miscarriage or especially perinatal death. Where the mother has not been able to mourn the death of the baby adequately, there can be a confusion in mother's mind between the dead and the live baby, compromising her recognition of the live baby's individuality and needs. For example, if the baby is of a different sex, this may not be easy to acknowledge, or the mother may be over-anxious about the baby's health and convey fears about survival that interfere in infant feeding and sleeping.

One striking clinical example of the impact of this kind of experience was work done by a colleague of mine with a surviving triplet. The other two babies had died in utero. This child proved very difficult to make contact with in therapy, and she and her mother seemed trapped in a chilly and unrewarding relationship, sadly without the potential help from the father who had abandoned them. However, Sandy, the surviving child, could convey something of her states of mind in drawing, and on one occasion drew a graveyard with three headstones which she clearly identified as belonging to herself and her siblings. This image helped her therapist to imagine the extent to which Sandy felt her life invaded by the reproachful ghosts of her siblings, seen as envying her the life denied to them and holding her prisoner in a place of death. This insight allowed the patient perhaps for the first time to realise that her guilt about being the survivor played a large part in her masochistic submission to these horrible, resentful, imagined siblings and set in train a less unequal struggle between the life and death instincts within her.

When a child dies in the family later on in life, the bereaved siblings have very complex feelings to bear. The balance of loving and hating feelings between the siblings before the death is the decisive factor in enabling such bereaved children to recover, alongside the resilience of their parents in coping with such a tragic loss. It is usually easier for children to deal with such losses, however painful the loss may be, than with the invisible babies of miscarriage or early infant death because the reality of their sibling's life will be acknowledged in the family and there will be memories, photographs and a spoken history which make the loss a shared and shareable experience.

Conclusions

The overview of the psychological significance of sibling relationships has inevitably not covered all aspects. For example, I have not focussed on the matter of gender—what difference does it make if we have brothers or sisters? What about the significance of sexual play and exploration between siblings? How can we distinguish between developmentally appropriate brother/sister feelings and more pathological features? As so often, literature serves to provide a resonant contrast: studying the sibling relationship in Shakespeare's *Measure for Measure* in comparison with that of the twins in *Twelfth Night* proved to be a fruitful way to explore this question. What became evident was the inner relationship to the parental couple that, in my view, provides the context for sibling relationships, a matrix in which the horizontal and vertical family relationships have a necessary connection (Rustin & Rustin in Coles, 2006). Klein wrote at one point about childhood sexual activity between siblings as having a creative potential, a stepping stone towards adolescent sexual development and a context in which sexual expression can be free from guilt, but such views are at odds with much current anxious preoccupation with the idea of any sexual activity between children being abusive. Coles (2003) and Mitchell (2003) have both aimed at theorising lateral relations of siblinghood which add to the oedipal parent–child structuring of the internal world, and which they argue are independent of oedipal dimensions. As will be evident, I am not persuaded of this despite strong agreement about the importance of siblings in our lives.

I will now attempt to summarise fundamental themes explored here. First, the idea that the existence of siblings is innate, a preconception (in Bion's terminology 1962) awaiting its realisation. They are always present in the mind, whether existing in external reality or not. Secondly, siblings are the object of passionate feelings of love and hate, and this is not only in connection with the context of sibling rivalry for parental affection and attention, a part of the wider oedipal drama, but also a site of our emotional lives with its own sources of energy. Thirdly, living with our siblings provides opportunities for shared experiences of many kinds—the sharing of the impact of parental pressures, the sharing of creative play and fantasy where long-term intimacy can be a preparation for both later friendships and love relationships, the sharing of family history and so on. Fourthly, the opportunity provided by siblings for multiple identifications and for the expansion of psychic life—we can, for example, move between being the baby and being the big one and we explore our bisexuality through relationships with our brothers and sisters. Fifthly, I have touched on some factors which introduce special risks and vulnerabilities such as the impact of a lost sibling, to which one should add the impact of a sibling with a disability, the meaning of multiple births, and the particular demands of relating to step-siblings and half-siblings in the many complex modern families. Linked to the issue of step-siblings are the experiences of children who are fostered or adopted which I have not discussed.

Whether we have actual siblings or not, our inner world is peopled by both friendly and unfriendly sibling figures. In psychotherapy, these can emerge in relation to thoughts and feelings about the therapist's other patients, and in an experience in the transference of the therapist as a sibling. I wondered, for instance, about Sophia's relationship with me being partly based on my being felt to be the longed-for absent sibling who could have been a playmate and could have shared the heavy load of her troubles with her parents. Intense feelings can also be experienced and worked through in relation to the therapist's own real family. When the patient becomes aware of the therapist's children as realities, by observing a pregnancy or by a chance meeting outside the clinical setting, this can become an all-too-real fact of life that may be very difficult to accommodate.

While sibling rivalry is an unavoidable element in our lives, the companionship of siblinghood is frequently felt to be a precious resource that overcomes our inescapable ambivalence. The intimacy of siblings and quasi-siblings (sometimes cousins, for example, can seem to be very close to sibling status) is for most of us the crucible in which we first learn how to make friends, how to get over quarrels, how to share, how to give and receive, and how to control our hatred and destructiveness with our peers. As with all intimate relationships, things can go wrong. From Jacob and Esau, and Cain and Abel onwards, the mental or physical violence that can erupt between siblings has been part of our human story. However, it seems to be evident that while siblings' feelings for each other are profoundly influenced by the parental context, there is also an independent factor. Our brothers and sisters are persons of value to us in their own right and are not only competitors for parental love. The facts of life in a family of whatever sort include the necessary acknowledgement of real and potential siblings and of our complex feelings about them; maybe the global facts of life in our 21st century interdependent world require some similar leap of imagination in the wider public sphere.

References

Adamo, S. (2006). *Il Compagno Immaginario. Scritti psicoanalitici.* Rome: Astrolabio Edizioni.

Adamo, S. M. G. & Rustin, M. (Eds.) (2001). Special Issue on Young Child Observation, *International Journal of Infant Observation*: 4(2).

Bick, E. (1968). The experience of skin in early object relations. *International Journal of Psychoanalysis, 49.*

Bion, W. R. (1962). *Learning from Experience.* London: Heineman.

Bion, W. R. (1970). *Attention and Interpretation.* London: Tavistock.

Briggs, A. (Ed.) (2004). *Surviving Space. Papers on infant observation.* London: Karnac Books.

Briggs, S. (1997). *Growth and Risk in Infancy.* London: Jessica Kingsley.

Canham, H. (2002). Group and Gang States of Mind. *Journal of Child Psychotherapy, 28* (2): 113–127.

Canham, H. & Emanuel, E. (2000). "Tied Together Feelings". *Journal of Child Psychotherapy, 26*(2): 281–302.

Coles, P. (2003). *The Importance of Sibling Relationships in Psychoanalysis.* London: Karnac Books.

Coles, P. (Ed.) (2006). *Sibling Relationships.* London: Karnac Books.

Cooper, H. (2005). In Magagna et al., 2005, pp. 42–56. (Originally published in the *International Journal of Infant Observation and Its Applications* 5:3: 69–82.)

Daws, D. (1989). *Through the Night.* London: Free Association Books.

Fraiberg, S. (Ed.) (1980). *Clinical Studies in Infant Mental Health.* London: Tavistock.

Freud, A. & Burlingham, D. (1874). *Infants without Families and Reports on the Hampstead Nurseries, 1939–45.* London: Hogarth.

Gretton, A. (2006). An account of a year's work with a mother and her 18-month-old son at risk of autism. *International Journal of Infant Observation, 9*(1): 21–34.

Hindle, J. (2007). Clinical research: a psychotherapeutic assessment model for siblings in care. *Journal of Child Psychotherapy* 33(1): 70–93.

Houzel, D. (2001). The "nest of babies" fantasy. *Journal of Child Psychotherapy, 27*(2): 125–138.

Lewin, V. (2004). *The Twin in the Transference.* London: Whurr.

Mitchell, J. (2003). *Siblings: Sex and Violence.* Cambridge: Polity Press.

Mitchell, J. (1960). In: P. Coles (Ed.), *Sibling Relationships.* London: Karnac Books.

Mc Ewan, I. (1996). *The Cement Garden.* London: Cape.

Money-Kyrle, R. E. (1978). *The Collected Papers of R. E. Money-Kyrle.* in D. Meltzer, (Ed.) with the assistance of E. O'Shaughnessy. Strath Tay, Perth: Clunie Press.

Pullman, P. (1997). *The Subtle Knife.* London: Scholastic.

Reid, M. (2003). Clinical research: the inner world of the mother and her new baby—born in the shadow of death. *Journal of Child Psychotherapy, 29*(2): 207–226.

Rustin, M. E. and Rustin, M. J. (2003). A new kind of friendship—an essay on Philip Pullman's *The Subtle Knife. Journal of Child Psychotherapy, 29*(2): 227–241.

Rustin, M. E. & Rustin, M. J. (2006). The Siblings of *Measure for Measure* and *Twelfth Night*'. In: P. Coles (Ed.), *Sibling Relationships.* London: Karnac Books.

Sherwin-White, S. (2007). Freud on brothers and sisters: a neglected topic. *Journal of Child Psychotherapy* 33(1): 4–20.

Sternberg, J. (2005). *Infant Observation at the Heart of Training.* London: Karnac Books.

Trowell, J. and Etchegoyan, A. (Eds.) (2002). *The Importance of Fathers: A Psychoanalytic Re-evaluation.* London: Routledge.

Tustin, F. (1972). *Autism and Childhood Psychosis.* London: Hogarth.

Waddell, M. & Williams, G. (1991). Reflections on perverse states of mind, *Free Associations,* 2: 203–213.

Note

1. An earlier version of this paper was given first at a conference at Santa Clara University, California (2005) and at the Guildford Centre for Psychotherapy (2006).

CONFERENCE 4

CHAPTER NINE

Twin development: Professor Alessandra Piontelli

Report by Vivienne Lewin

The first Siblings Conference was on April 21st, when Alessandra Piontelli had been unable to attend as planned. We were pleased, therefore, to invite Professor Piontelli back to present her material at an additional half-day conference.

The presentation consisted of film of ultra-sound scans of twins in utero followed by later film as infants and toddlers. The morning was an interactive event rather than a lecture, and the audience was engaged and questioning. Many members of the audience acknowledged that they were either twins, or the parents of twins.

Professor Piontelli started with the biological distinction between monozygotic and dizygotic twins:

Monozygotic twins are the result of the fertilisation of one egg by one sperm. The fertilised egg then divides and this may happen at different stages in the very early development of the embryo.

i.) where this division occurs very early, the resulting foetuses will have 2 placentas and two dividing membranes.
ii.) with later division of the embryo, the two foetuses will share the same placenta and dividing membranes. These twins are at risk from twin-twin transfusion syndrome and if one twin dies, the other would then be at risk of brain damage or death.
iii.) still later, the embryos will share one placenta and one amniotic sac. These twins face the highest risk of strangulation by the umbilical cord.

Dizygotic twins result from the fertilisation of two eggs by two sperms. Risk is minimised by the preference for all twins to be born at 37 weeks.

The first film showed the splitting of the fertilised egg. Piontelli pointed out that the splitting of the ovum was not a neat or even split; one split-off embryo was likely to be bigger than the other and more favoured right from the start. She stressed that from the beginning, monozygotic twins are NOT identical. There are many differences between them. Neither do twins have an equal environment as they develop in utero. It is not known why a fertilised egg divides, and Piontelli suggested that it is not familial but rather that there might be a defect in the membrane or a cohesion of cells that leads to the splitting of the fertilised ovum.

In film of foetuses in utero moving, we observed that by 20 weeks they move a lot, showing cycles of activity and of rest. Later in development, the cycles cluster more, and we can then observe proper sleep in the foetuses. During sleep, the foetuses move frequently, and a remnant of this can be observed in neonates as well. Whether foetuses were asleep or awake, Piontelli differentiated between their general movements and localised movements. It is only later in development that movements become voluntary. General movements in the foetus prevent adhesion to the wall of the uterus and promote the growth of the central nervous system, muscles etc.

Looking at foetuses at 10 weeks after conception, we observed that one twin was considerably smaller than the other and the membrane between them was interrupted. Although they were moving, they were not awake and the movements were involuntary. They could, however, stimulate each other by these general movements. Each twin would have its own cycles of activity, as do singletons. The mother of these twins, on seeing the scan, referred to the bigger foetus as the "vampire" and the smaller one as the "victim". These names persisted after the twins were born, and later in the presentation we observed them as toddlers.

Wakefulness begins at 36/37 weeks. Piontelli distinguished wakefulness from consciousness. It is not clear when consciousness starts, as the foetus has no cortex for the first half of the pregnancy. After birth, the neonate also moves in its sleep and responds without consciousness at times.

Piontelli pointed out that it is important that we attribute meaning to things the infant does after birth in order to try to understand our children from our own experience. But meaning attribution is not essential before birth as the foetus is not yet a social being in a social environment. Foetal social activity does occur in utero as well as some preparation for social life after birth, but this is not the same as a functional social life. Twins have a bodily sense and, therefore, respond to their environment and to each other. In a film of identical twin foetuses we saw that the reaction between them was not social but reactive. We can see twins reacting to each other in utero, but this does not constitute awareness of the other twin. Awareness of each other occurs some time after birth.

At this point I wondered about proto-mental activity and sensate memories in the foetuses, each with a functioning, if immature, cortex before birth. Given that newborn infants respond discriminatingly to sounds of mother's voice, music and to smells of mother and her milk, and search out mother's face/eyes in preference to another adult's (Proner, 2000), I believe infants are born already relating, if in a primitive way, to others who are familiar to them from prenatal times—mother with whom they are familiar from their experience in the womb, a twin with whom the womb has been shared and who would have impinged on them in all sorts of ways.

Piontelli suggested that voice recognition begins later in pregnancy, as the foetus is preparing for birth. At first, the foetus responds to sounds, including mother's voice. The capacity to recognise sound starts later, at birth, when meeting with real people. In utero, foetuses also respond to the different diets of the mother, which they sample first in the amniotic fluid, then, after birth, in the mother's milk, setting the pattern for acceptance of different diets.

In a film of mono-chorionic (shared placenta) twins we noted how a startle response in one twin put in motion general activity, like jumping, in the other. The jumping twin created some laughter in the audience. Piontelli suggested that this level of responsive activity decreases as pregnancy and development proceeds, but it is retained to some extent in the neonate, as well as in adults in the first phase of falling asleep, when we suddenly jerk.

Mono-chorionic twins tend to create more anxiety because in the event of the death of one twin, the surviving twin is at risk of brain damage or death. Piontelli believes that pregnant women are generally bombarded with anxieties, and this is especially so if they are carrying twins. A twin pregnancy is a very public event and this would add to the distress of the parents in situations when one or both twins are lost. The anxiety about caring for two babies is extended to prenatal life and the mother may be very anxious about her foetuses. As twins do not share the same prenatal environment, study of the effects of mother's anxiety on the foetuses is not possible.

Although size discrepancy between twins in early pregnancy is long lasting, the smaller twin foetus may catch up by 20 weeks. A film of monozygotic twins showed a considerable difference in size between the twin foetuses, and in newborn twins, but Piontelli pointed out that sometimes the smaller twin may not be disadvantaged, and may be more alert than the bigger one. The activity we were seeing on the video indicating the reaction between the twins was not a complicated social one. It was, instead, a reactive one.

We then observed a mother with her new dizygotic twins. For a mother of twins, coping with two infants may seem to be overwhelming, so in choosing one twin as her favourite, she creates a situation akin to that of having a singleton baby on whom she can focus. Additionally, twins are usually born by Caesarean section, and this may also affect how mother feels about her babies. This mother wondered how she could choose between her babies, looking from twin to twin. Eventually she showed a clear preference for the less beautiful twin. The non-favourite twin was always fed by a neighbour, while mother fed the preferred baby. It was noticeable that the preferred baby was more at ease and gazed at mother during feeding, while the neighbour-fed twin seemed to be detached and rather stiff. However, the neighbour-fed baby later turned out to be more sociable than the mother-fed twin, and the darling of his teachers.

It is difficult to draw inferences from these sorts of situations, though one might speculate about the development of each twin in relation to the various factors in their environment. Piontelli pointed out that feeding was not the only modality for expressions of preference, and that infants also affect the relationship by expressing their needs. She added that fathers of twins are thrown into the paternal role faster than those of singletons, as caring for two infants simultaneously is so much more demanding.

Family reactions to twins vary enormously. We observed film of a family in which there were already two older children, and where mother had contemplated a termination, as she was concerned about her ability to cope. In the event she decided against termination, and this would have affected her phantasies and expectations relating to the twins. We saw the big brother holding his baby twin-brothers proudly and comfortably, while father seemed disheartened and overwhelmed in having to manage two new babies. One twin was very vocal, trying to engage his twin, while the other was shy and timid, looking rather anxious about his twin's approaches to him.

In a follow up to the scan of the "vampire" and "victim" twin foetuses we had observed earlier, we saw the twins as toddlers interacting. The "victim" twin had grown considerably and was an active and interested baby. Mother repeatedly accused the "vampire" twin of grabbing toys from the "victim" twin, despite the fact that it was clear from the film that the reverse was happening. The "victim" twin wanted everything and mother encouraged him to take it. Eventually the "vampire" twin resorted to a pacifier as if defeated.

I felt it was clear that mother had a preformed view of each of her infants, based on their appearance in the ultra-sound film, and that she persisted in her view despite the actual behaviour of the twins and evidence to the contrary. So we see a splitting in the projections of the mother, reflecting her prejudices and expectations in this situation. This may be a way of trying to cope with the overwhelming demand from two same-age infants, with each twin coming to represent a different aspect of mother's emotional connection with them.

In a film of premature infants, born at 24 weeks, we saw how important bonding with the infants was to a father whose poor fertility had required fertility treatment. Here we saw a father feeling very at home with and loving towards his twins. The smaller twin was more outgoing and loved the camera. The larger one was suspicious and hid away. At six months, we observed them interacting together. The smaller twin was very vocal and trying to engage his twin brother, the other twin again looked away, appearing very uncomfortable and afraid.

Film of dizygotic, different-sex twins demonstrated the persistence after birth of traits that had been observed in utero. The girl foetus was more active while the boy tended to rest. After birth the boy sat passively observing his twin sister as she lay down wriggling and actively kicking her legs. Father said, "the girl does, the boy observes." She was perpetually moving, though at one point the boy kicked his legs a little as if to emulate his very active twin sister. Imitation was something we saw in several of the films, some twins adopting a second-hand engagement with their environment by imitating the explorations of the more active and curious twin.

Temperamental differences in twins were highlighted in a sequence of film showing twin babies playing with a new toy—a sponge. The more outgoing twin was much more adventurous with the sponge although it was for him a new object. Mother threw the sponge along the floor and the adventurous baby raced after and explored it while the other baby crawled away. When mother pushed the sponge towards him, he pushed it away. Eventually he dared to approach it, but only through his twin brother who had somehow detoxified the new object. We later watched as the adventurous twin explored the content of Piontelli's handbag, taking each thing out in turn, while his twin brother watched him. It seemed that the timid twin did not dare find things himself, but could only handle them through his twin whom he copied. The adventurous twin seemed to have transformed the strange new thing into something safer for him. In a later sequence, the adventurous twin plays with a shoe-cleaning machine with interest and gusto while his twin watches fearfully, sitting stiffly behind him.

Piontelli stated that temperament in infants is present prenatally, and at three months after birth there are strong temperamental differences between twins. She stressed that the intra-uterine environment **is** an environment and will, therefore, affect development. Mother's attitude will also affect the twins, but there are many important factors, including innate factors.

Piontelli spoke about twins who had been separated at birth, a subject that has generated massive funding and has seized the public imagination. However, she suggested, the research is flawed in its focus on similarities rather than differences. Its aim is to prove the identicality of monozygotic twins, but as twins are never identical and do not share the same intrauterine or familial environment; it is based on a false premise. We saw in the film of the "vampire" and "victim" how much the parental perceptions of each twin differ, and this will create for each of the twins a unique emotional and developmental environment.

An ultrasound film showed a new pair of monozygotic twins in very close proximity. The separating membrane was very thin, as a result of which they would have had much closer contact in utero. After birth the twins were seen to relate to each other in preference to relating to mother and father. We observed this close interaction between them, as one kissed the other. In the bath together, they ignored mother and Piontelli, and the bath toys, preferring to engage with each other in a mutually erotic encounter. Mother said she felt excluded and she left the twins to get on with it.

Later we saw them aged five years, wrestling, very tactile, again in mutually erotic play. It was reported that even though each twin had his own bed, they would move into the same bed, and were later observed masturbating each other. The twins seemed so wrapped up in each other that they were oblivious to the camera, and in their own world. The intimacy between them was sexualised and excluded mother. The family attitude was said to be very liberal and the parents did not attempt to intervene in this intense inter-twin relationship. Mother apparently blamed their Caesarean birth for what she considered to be a lack of imprinting with her twins. They were very unruly and later teachers expressed concern about them. But Piontelli stressed that they did manage to learn at school and make progress.

In contrast, the next film showed monozygotic twins interacting strongly with their mother. They were geared towards adults rather than each other. We observed mother talking to one twin, smiling at him. The other twin became restless and started to cry. Mother noticed and moved over to the crying twin and started to talk to him and smile at him. He calmed and responded brightly, while the first twin got restless and began to cry. We observed the same twins a few months later, interacting. One was trying to squash the other, lying on top of him, pushing him down, crying as he did so, as if to say "get rid of him, Mama". Mother says, "What can I do with two?"

The closeness of another pair of twins at two months showed one sucking and nuzzling the other, who is yawning. Three months later we see them holding hands and clearly interacting with each other. They were very tactile with each other. When they were laid face to face, they looked at each other searchingly. Piontelli suggested that their tentative relationship with each other, looking at each other, touching, began at four months rather than with the earlier interaction we had observed, but which she did not regard as a truly social relationship.

In response to a question, Professor Piontelli discussed how it comes about that twins seem to act identically. One mechanism is imitation; we had seen earlier the "vampire" twin who was really a very shy child, imitating the "victim" twin. However, this behaviour is based on imitation rather than any notion of the twins behaving identically as a result of genetic predisposition.

The accent in twin development now tends to be on individuation rather than on studying similarity. Twins have to find a balance between their intertwined relationship and their separateness, while negotiating the exclusivity of the twin relationship. However, Piontelli ended by stressing cultural differences, showing two pairs of twin men, one pair in India and the other in Togo, who had married one woman.

I was troubled by this apparently amicable and acceptable solution, as it suggested that twins may be regarded as one person divided into two halves, rather than two distinct people. One also wonders what the wife made of this arrangement.

Viewing Piontelli's films provided a fascinating window on the links between pre and postnatal life in twins. The audience responded warmly to this and there were many questions, all answered attentively. There was, however, little attempt to link our observations from the films with psychoanalytic understanding of development, particularly in twins. Piontelli was also careful not to lay any blame or make judgements about what we were observing, which led to a feeling that we could not draw any conclusions from what we had observed.

I was aware of, and commented on, the similarities between the very intertwined twin boys who excluded parental influence and Bill and Bert (Burlingham, 1952)—a pair of highly problematic twins who exhibited a profound inter-twin entanglement and mutually erotic and aggressive behaviour. Bill and Bert's difficulties proved to be lifelong and seriously affected their other relationships and ability to function productively in the world. With the pair we observed it was as if the parent's laissez-faire attitude had permeated the thinking about them and had veiled any awareness of the need for a parental structure to enable these twins to face the ordinary obstacles in development and in particular the negotiation of the Oedipus Complex. I was left feeling concerned about how we view twin relationships, particularly the developmental potential between twins, and between each twin and its parents, as I have discussed at length in my book (Lewin, 2004).

References

Burlingham, D. T. (1952). *Twins. A Study of Three Pairs of Identical Twins*. London: Imago.

Lewin, V. (2004). *The Twin in the Transference*. London: Whurr.

Proner, K. (2000). Protomental synchrony: some thoughts on the earliest identification processes in a neonate. *The International Journal of Infant Observation, 3*: 55–63.

INDEX

For Product Safety Concerns and Information please contact our EU
representative GPSR@taylorandfrancis.com
Taylor & Francis Verlag GmbH, Kaufingerstraße 24, 80331 München, Germany

www.ingramcontent.com/pod-product-compliance
Ingram Content Group UK Ltd.
Pitfield, Milton Keynes, MK11 3LW, UK
UKHW022202190926
475702UK00003B/158
* 9 7 8 0 3 6 7 3 2 6 9 3 7 *